New product development

A practical workbook for improving performance

Ian Barclay, Zoe Dann and Philip Holroyd

THE INSTITUTE OF
OPERATIONS
MANAGEMENT

CRC Press
Boca Raton Boston New York Washington, DC

OXFORD AUCKLAND BOSTON JOHANNESBURG MELBOURNE NEW DELHI

Butterworth-Heinemann
Linacre House, Jordan Hill, Oxford OX2 8DP
225 Wildwood Avenue, Woburn, MA 01801-2041
A division of Reed Educational and Professional Publishing Ltd

 A member of the Reed Elsevier plc group

First published 2000

Published in association with the Institute of Operations Management

Published in North and South America by CRC Press LLC, 2000 Corporate Blvd,
NW Boca Raton FL 33431, USA

© Reed Educational and Professional Publishing Ltd 2000

The authors have asserted their moral rights.

British Library Cataloguing in Publication Data
A catalogue record for this book is available from the British Library

Library of Congress Cataloguing in Publication Data
New product development: a practical workbook and
  software package/edited by Ian Barclay, Zoe Dann, Philip Holroyd.
  p. cm.
  A both paper and Microsoft Office Access based package.
  Accompanying CD-ROM contains flowcharts and ATM (Assessment Tool and Methodology).
  Includes index.
  System requirements for accompanying computer disc:
  ISBN 0-8493-2385-1 (alk. paper)
  1. New products. 2. Production management. 3. New products Case studies. I. Barclay, Ian 1943–.
  II. Dann, Zoe. 1966– . III. Holroyd, Philip, 1931–.
  TS170.I53   99-39003
  658.5' 75–dc21   CIP

Butterworth-Heinemann ISBN 0 7506 4998 4
CRC Press ISBN 0-8493-2385-1
CRC Press order number: WP2385

Typeset by Best-set Typesetters Ltd, Hong Kong
Printed and bound in Great Britain by Biddles, Guildford and Kings Lynn

New product development

CARLISLE

This book is due for return on or before the last date shown below.

* Ask	for CD Rom	at counter*
2-7 OCT 2004 CD Taken.		
22 DEC 2006		
2 5 NOV 2008		

Contents

Appendices   **127**

Acknowledgements

We would like to thank the following individuals and organisations that gave us considerable help and support in this work.

Individuals

Dr Jenny Poolton for developing the original concept and working with the companies.

Dr David Waring (Kodak Ltd) for his support on the grant steering committee.

Dr Tony Blythe (BICC Cables Ltd) for his support on the grant steering committee.

In the Technology Management Group

Paul Otterson for his persistence in making the ATM work.
Paul Haynes for the design and development of the ATM disk.
Neil Weekes for his work in defining the style of the workbook.
Brenda Edwards for organising us.

At Liverpool John Moores University

The Teaching and Learning Unit for preparing the CD-ROM and especially Gareth Price, Dave Kennedy, Andrew Hooper and Peter Kelly.

Companies

BBA Friction Ltd.
BICC Cables Ltd.
Continental Sports Ltd.
Engineering Ltd (they will know who they are!)

J C Bamford Excavators Ltd.
Lantor (UK) Ltd.
Try & Lilly Ltd.
Wylex Ltd.
Murata Company, Japan.
Nissan Technical Centre, Japan.
Sony Company, Japan.
Sumitomo Company, Japan.

Organisations

Liverpool John Moores University and especially its School of Engineering.
LJMU's Technology Management Group staff for their support and encouragement.
Engineering and Physical Sciences Research Council for their support.
University of Liverpool Engineering Faculty.

Introducing the workbook

This workbook is the result of many years of practical involvement and applied research (including a major Engineering and Physical Sciences Research Council grant) in the evaluation and improvement of the new product development (NPD) activities and process. The recent work involved detailed collaboration with ten companies from a wide cross-section of UK industry and four Japanese companies in Japan.

The workbook aims to help practitioners assess and improve both their NPD activities and the NPD process. It is designed to allow company personnel to develop improvements to the processes and methods that are specific and relevant to their own company. Anyone involved in the development of new products, as an individual or a part of a team, will find this workbook useful.

Product development is a complex and risky business and there are no universal panaceas that will guarantee success. As such, we do not offer composite solutions, rather a flexible approach to the problems and issues that companies face when generating new business via the development and launch of new or modified products.

Philosophy and rationale

The basic premise of the workbook is that products and their development process and its management are unique to each company. Company 'history' also influences the approach to NPD and how it might be (or has been) operated and improved. Each company's starting point and needs are unique and any improvement work must be tailored to suit. For this reason, the workbook is directive and not prescriptive. It will allow you to compare your position relative to best practice for product development in a similar area. It will also present alternative approaches to improving your NPD activities and process, thus allowing you to focus on those that are most appropriate to your situation, need and preference.

The approach taken is to try to accommodate and address the issues and problems described above. Companies adopt specific development approaches for a variety of reasons, not all of them immediately obvious. The more successful companies address product development as an important strategic issue and a business process that demands constant attention. The workbook blends tried and tested research evidence with practical experience and the observation of people involved in NPD. It may be used in the following ways:

- **As an educational tool**: for general awareness and as an introduction to the key issues and findings relating to the development activities and process.
- **As a practical application package**: for
  - specific or general improvement of the overall NPD process;
  - pre-development assessment and evaluation;
  - post-development assessment and evaluation;
  - success/failure comparison;
  - benchmarking good and/or appropriate practice.
- **Individual or team mode**: the workbook may be used by an individual or a team. This latter mode is particularly useful for resolving problems.

Aims of the workbook

In developing the workbook, we conducted a survey of practitioners to define its scope, content and approach. It focuses on the practical management and improvement of a company's NPD activities and process. We have adopted a variety of approaches, ranging from systematic to more intuitive, 'gut-feeling' ones. This reflects both the different types of NPD environments that exist and individual users' styles and preferences. While there must be 'theoretical' content, the primary aim is to promote action in a 'user friendly way'. This is achieved by:

- Keeping it simple in content and approach.
- Making it short and sharp in style.
- Segmenting it for 'dipping' into specific sections.
- Presenting the assessment tool and methodology in both paper and Microsoft Access form (see Part III).

The workbook will help to improve development performance by providing both product and non-product specific improvement methods, reviewing learning from previous product developments and by evaluating future product development needs. To do this, it addresses improvement by:

- Incremental and/or continuous change approach.
- Radical change approach.
- Product or general process review.
- Both systematic and intuitive approaches.
- Problem resolution and opportunity taking.

An overview of the structure and content

This section is a general guide to the workbook.

Part I: The 'educational' package

Part I of the workbook introduces, in a practical form, the current 'theory' relating to NPD and its improvement.

1. Product development: its context and content

This section places NPD within the context of the new competitive environment and companies' responses to these issues. It addresses the question of 'how new is new?' and the related problems of product and market complexities. It also introduces models of the NPD activities and process that are used throughout the practical application sections. Finally there is an introduction to our assessment tool and methodology.

2. New product development trends

The competitive environment of the world has changed dramatically in the 1980s and 1990s. The pace of change has increased with increasing market fragmentation, variety and complexity. This section describes and explains the trends in NPD over this period. The key trends include:

- NPD being established as a key element in a company's strategic plans.
- The drive to reduce time to market and increase 'right first time' developments.
- The increasing need for teams, high-quality team leaders and team training.
- The introduction and use of product development guides and procedures.
- Increased and more sophisticated use of NPD performance measures.
- Introduction and use of post-development reviews.
- Education in and understanding of the total NPD process.

The trends that are driving changes in both NPD activities and process provide valuable lessons that have been obtained from detailed research work. Most of these lessons are common sense, but they are proven common sense. This section also reviews the work done in trying to differentiate between successful and less successful products.

3. Strategic issues in improving NPD performance

Having a clearly defined and appropriate NPD strategy has emerged as one of the key lessons from all the research evidence on success in NPD. Because NPD is emerging as a key business growth driver, addressing its strategic dimension will become even more important. This section takes some of the more accessible strategic theories and relates them to a company's NPD needs.

4. Evaluating product development performance

The desire to improve both the development performance and product development success rates has been an issue that has been constantly addressed by both researchers and practitioners. Improvement in development success rates and the performance of the overall process are inextricably linked. Yet it is only recently that a clear distinction has been drawn between managing programmes to completion (internal performance) and the acceptance of the product in the market-place (external performance). This section looks at the problems of measuring performance from the perspectives of how to actually measure it (performance measurement systems) and what to measure (performance metrics).

5. Improving product development performance

Relating market performance back to the next generation of products is extremely difficult. This creates problems when trying to improve the overall development performance and often leads to piecemeal approaches or the introduction of methods from other activities (e.g. total quality management). The best way to avoid this is by adopting an overall and strategic approach to improving performance. Performance improvement covers:

- **Internal efficiency**. These improvement measures are much easier to establish and monitor (programme cost, person hours expended, etc.). Clearly, ultimate product and market impact are affected by the development cost and time to market.

- **External effectiveness**. Better analysis of market-place need, better project evaluation, assessment and selection and clearer market-place related interim measures (profit cannot be measured during the development process).

The basic problem when assessing improvement activities is one of immediacy. Internal efficiency lends itself to short-term manipulation and impact whereas external effectiveness does not. Very few companies are sophisticated enough or even willing to conduct a detailed development review and then translate this into improved front-end performance. This balance between internal/external and front-end/back-end process is discussed in more detail.

Having a clearly defined development strategy gives the improvement work a direction and focus. Taking a holistic view ensures that all elements are included and the focus is placed where it is most needed or will be most beneficial. Small incremental changes, as opposed to radical ones, are the preferred route for improving development performance. The best companies recognise the importance of the product development process and work hard to improve it.

Part II: Practical application

Part II of the workbook addresses the practical issues of improving NPD performance. It describes the benefits of a structured and focused review of development strategy, activities and process. Conducting a post-development review on a specific development is an excellent way of learning about the good, mediocre and bad aspects of a development environment. Also, the successful/less successful products evaluation process that is introduced gives clear indications of the factors leading to success.

Part II is divided into three sections:

- 6. Application of NPD strategy.
- 7. Measuring development performance.
- 8. Improving development performance.

Part III: The assessment tool and methodology

This explains how the ATM may be used in:

- Retrospective or post-development evaluation.
- Successful/less successful comparison.
- Predictive assessment for a new development.

- Team based assessment.
- Benchmarking.

The Microsoft Access-based assessment tool and methodology is included here.

Part IV: Case studies

We have included case studies that show the practical realisation of the lessons that have been learnt and developed. The case studies are:

- J C Bamford Excavators Ltd.
- BBA Friction Ltd.
- Continental Sports Ltd.
- Engineering Ltd (a confidential case study).
- Lantor (UK) Ltd.
- Try & Lilly Ltd.
- Wylex Ltd.

Part V: Useful contacts and addresses

At the end of the workbook are listed some relevant organisations.

The CD-ROM

The CD-ROM contained within the workbook has the following items on it:

The flowcharts found in the appendices

The flowcharts in the appendices are also found on the CD-ROM. If you click on any part of a particular flowchart, it will guide you to the relevant section of the workbook or give you advice as to how to proceed.

The ATM

The ATM is contained on the CD-ROM and can be completed here. For further details, please see Sections 9 and 10.

General terminology

As help in using the workbook, an explanation of some of the terminology used throughout it is presented here:

- **NPD performance level**: your success rate in developing new products. This can be either internal (budget, time, etc), or external (profit, customer satisfaction, etc) or both.
- **Performance measurement process and system**: the process or system by which you measure the development performance.
- **Performance metrics**: the actual measures used in evaluating your product development performance.
- **Overall review**: a comprehensive review of all aspects of your product development activities and process.
- **Integrating activities**: our model of the internal environment relating to your product development activities (see Appendix 1).
- **Development process**: our model of the product development process (see Appendix 2).
- **Assessment Tool and Methodology (ATM)**: the tool and methodology that has been developed for carrying out a structured review and evaluation of your product development activities and process (see Chapters 9 and 10).
- **Improvement focus**: the focus of the improvement assessment and work programme.
- **Improvement targets**: the specific, measurable targets of the improvement programme.

Part I

The 'educational' package

1

Product development: its context and content

1.1 Issues and problems in new product development

A major source of successful competitive advantage for companies in the future will be the consistent and successful development of new and modified products. However, batch sizes, repeat orders and product life cycles are all reducing as product variety increases (because of niche market penetration). For a group of consumer products introduced in the 1920s, the average time from introduction to peak production was approximately 28 years. For a similar group of products introduced in the 1960–70s, this time had reduced to 10 years. This is a trend that is set to continue and poses major problems for product development practitioners. In our 1987 survey of 149 UK engineering-based manufacturing companies we found that the average product life cycle was 12 years and the average development time was 22 months. We repeated the survey in 1996 and these figures had become eight years and 15 months respectively. Estimates suggest that the number of new products launched in the next five years will be twice that of the last five years. This explosion in product development will account for a 40% increase in sales turnover and 30% increase in company profits.

Thus the ability to produce a steady flow of successful new products consistently is one of the key factors in corporate success. However, only about 10% of all new products developed make a significant contribution to corporate profits. When the research evidence on success and failure in product development is examined, failure rates have remained at about 30% for the last 60 years. Either companies are not getting any better at the new product development (NPD) process or, more likely, they are becoming more expert and critical in the approach to the measurement of success.

Our work with our collaborating companies in the 1980s and 1990s indicates that the product development process is seen as increasingly important. In the 1987 survey, only 40% of surveyed companies had any form of product development guide or procedure. In the 1996 survey, this figure had reached over 90%.

One final introductory comment concerns all the research work that has been conducted into what is a complex and highly uncertain process. Although a large number of detailed research studies have looked at all aspects of product innovation, little of the knowledge gained in these programmes has been transferred directly to the practitioner community. The reasons for this are:

- **Unawareness**: only 8% of those companies we surveyed had heard of the key research studies presented to them.
- **Generalised output**: the results were too general to be applied easily and were rarely in a form that allowed for ease of interpretation and application by individual companies.
- **Retrospective research work**: it is fairly easy to define the factors that make a product a success or failure once the results are known, but it is extremely difficult to predict success.

Three fundamental principles emerge from all the past research evidence on NPD:

- **Company-specific issues**: there is no universally applicable panacea or solution to the NPD problems that exist.
- **'Tailoring' the process**: a company's development environment (both internal and external) is unique to that company. Improvement processes have to be 'tailored' to suit the specific circumstances.
- **Things change**: especially in product development terms and what works today may not be appropriate for the next generation of products. What has been discarded today may be key to the future.

1.2   How new is new?

The term new product development is all embracing and ranges from products that are totally new to the world to minor modifications. Booze, Allen and Hamilton defined six categories of 'new products' as shown in Table 1.1. Some of these developments might involve no change to the actual

Table 1.1. Booze, Allen and Hamilton's newness

Definition	Nature
New to the world	Entirely new
New product lines	New market entry
Additional lines	Supplements
Improvements	Additional 'value'
Re-positioning	Into new markets
Cost reductions	For same performance

Table 1.2. The 'newness' of product development

Development type	% of total
Establishes whole new category	Nil
First type on the market in existing category	2
Significant improvement on existing technology	12
Modest improvement/update to existing product	86

Table 1.3. The key properties of the developments

Key property	% of total
More user friendly	32
Safer or more reliable	16
More flexible	11
Time saving	9
Miscellaneous (20 categories)	32

product itself. The results of a recent survey of some 5,000 product developments described the nature of the product development effort (Table 1.2).

It is clear from this study and from our experience with collaborating companies that small, incremental changes in products are the rule and major product changes the exception.

Some questions to ask

What is the ratio of your major and incremental developments?
It is worth knowing, as different approaches are probably needed.

Can you interchange between radical and incremental changes?
Your staff need to be motivated to do both, the problem being that it is the large, radical developments that attract status.

An even more telling reflection on the trends influencing product development work today is the 'key property' analysis of the above product newness as shown in Table 1.3. The emergence of the consumer is one of the most influential trends of recent times. This has been taken into account in designing and developing the workbook.

Some questions to ask

Are you trying to target specific customer requirements?
You should be, especially with incremental changes.

Do you have direct contact with the end-user (who is not necessarily the customer)?
You must find ways of achieving this objective.

1.3   Product/market complexity

At the heart of any NPD improvement work is the relationship between the product and its market placement. Clark and Fujimito published an article describing this relationship in terms of a matrix based on the complexity of the internal product structure (number of components, connections, etc) and the complexity of the product user interface (number of performance criteria, its 'fit' with the user, etc). We refer to these as structural complexity and functional complexity respectively and their relationship is shown in Fig. 1.1.

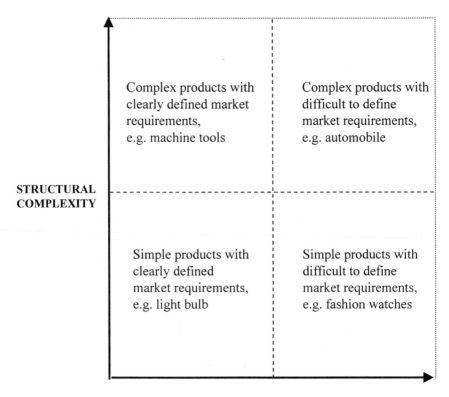

FUNCTIONAL COMPLEXITY

1.1 The structural and functional complexities relationship.

The theory behind this is that as developments move towards placement in the upper right area of the matrix, so the development's complexity and its degree of difficulty increase. As a result, you are more likely to have to use complexity-resolving activities such as teams, formal methods, etc. However, this is only part of the complexity considerations. While the Clark and Fujimito model holds well for the general environment, our research shows that three other key complexity measures play a vital role when addressing a specific development. These are:

- **Product newness**: the degree to which various aspects are new to the company.
- **Programme complexity**: the size of the programme and its inter-relatedness.
- **Commercial constraints**: the limitations imposed by commercial considerations.

1.4 Modelling the development environment

In order to understand and thus adjust a company's product development activities, a model that is a reasonable representation of the NPD environment is required. The word 'reasonable' is important here as many theoretical models exist. Some are specific, focusing on a particular element and some are general. The problem is that the two extremes are of little use for practical application. The workbook describes a model (see Appendix 1) that is a blend of the two and also robust enough for practical application. This model is used throughout the workbook.

1.5 Modelling the development process

As with the development activities, many models exist for the development process and we adopted a similar approach in developing our own. The outcome is that we now use the 13-step process model shown in Appendix 2. This model is used throughout the workbook.

Some questions to ask

Which of the activities and process stages do you use?
Not all companies use them all, so do not be afraid to leave some out. However, do check whether any of the ones you do not use should, in fact, be included.

1.6   What does the practitioner want/need?

The final deliberation in preparing the workbook was around the question of what practitioners would want or need. Our New Product Club (a club for NPD practitioners) and a detailed questionnaire survey were used to determine this. The results are as follows. It should be:

- Relevant to their specific needs.
- Fairly comprehensive.
- Capable of offering a variety of approaches.
- Both educational and action-oriented.
- Capable of being used in total or selectively.
- Able to 'force' the development and implementation of action plans.

All these points have all been addressed in producing the workbook.

1.7   The assessment tool and methodology: bringing it all together

The assessment tool and methodology (ATM) is the practical assessment and evaluation tool that brings all the above theory together and this process is shown diagrammatically in Appendix 3.

The ATM measures the complexities and newness of a product and relates them to the NPD integrating activities and process. The detail of using the ATM is given in Part III of the workbook and it may be used by companies in a variety of ways:

- **Post-development review**: by reviewing a completed development, the good and bad aspects of it may be clearly identified and appropriate action(s) taken to improve future developments.
- **Success/failure comparison**: running the ATM on both successful and less successful developments allows the key differences to be identified and action to be taken.
- **Appropriate practice benchmarking**: the authors are building a database of successful developments to allow appropriate practice to be identified and accessed.
- **Pre-development assessment**: the ATM presents a structured and focused methodology for detailed assessment of the specific needs of a proposed development. It is useful in identifying key issues and resolving points of potential conflict or problems.

1.8   References and indicative reading

Product Development Performance: Strategy, Organisation, and Management in the World Auto Industry, K B Clark and T Fujimito, Harvard Business School Press, Boston, MA (1991).

Winning at New Products: Accelerating the Process from Idea to Launch, R G Cooper, Second Edition, Cambridge, MA (1993).

New Products Management (5th edn), M Crawford, Richard D Irwin, Chicago (1997).

New Product Development for the 1980's, Booze, Allen and Hamilton, Booze, Allen and Hamilton, Inc., New York (1982).

2

New product development trends

2.1 Introduction

This section looks at the key trends that are influencing product development activities and their effect on success and failure rates. The information is derived from detailed company and general literature surveys conducted by Liverpool John Moores University's Technology Management Group.

2.2 General trends

The market life span of products is decreasing and their rate of development is predicted to double every five years. Thus the production of a steady stream of new products that customers will desire and appreciate is a key factor in maintaining and improving competitive advantage. Since the mid-1980s the industrial sector has sought such competitive advantage by improving production efficiency, cost effectiveness, quality systems and so on. It is now at a stage where customer-driven product development provides one of the key factors separating success from failure. Excellence in this area is essential if local, national and global markets are to be captured.

The global economy produces some interesting product development effects with markets fragmenting and mass production becoming less important than mass customisation (satisfying the individual consumer's 'emotive' feel for the product). Customers now also buy on more than price and performance. They require the 'product package' to include a substantial service element. Indeed, the phrase 'manufacturing as a service' now applies equally well to component manufacturers as it does to the more service-based companies.

As markets emerge, the actual products that are developed by competing companies using common technologies tend to become undifferentiated and of similar performance (visit any consumer appliance store).

Hence a major competitive advantage in the future will be the ability to create and exploit the 'emotives' in the product; that is the intangible aspects that make the product 'the one for me'.

In summary, the key trends include the following:

- **Competitive advantage**: product development being a key determinant of competitive advantage for both companies and nations.
- **A strategic issue**: product development becoming a major strategic issue for companies.
- **Increasing activity**: the rate of introduction of new products to double every five years.
- **Reducing development time**: to reduce in line with the increasing introduction rate.
- **Company-specific approaches**: each company will need to address the issues that are specific to their own internal and external environments and to develop appropriate NPD practices.
- **Continuous improvement**: in NPD performance.

Some questions to ask

Do you recognise these trends in your environment?
If they are not there already, they will be in the short-term future.

Do you have plans to address them?
If yes, then good; if not, the workbook will help you.

2.3   The major trends

An overview

The specific trends and the organisational responses to them are presented in Fig. 2.1.

Number of developments

The number of new products being developed at any one time by a company obviously depends on the nature of the products and the market in which they are placed. The results of the authors' 1996 survey are shown in Table 2.1.

These figures are almost identical to figures from a similar survey conducted by the authors five years earlier. Taken in isolation, these results appear to contradict the opening remarks about the increasing number of products being developed. However, if we look at lead-times and life-cycle

COMPETITIVE PRESSURE

ORGANISATION'S RESPONSE

INCREASING

* COMPETITION
* VARIETY
* DIFFERENTIATION

RIGHT FIRST TIME PHILOSOPHY

REDUCED DEVELOPMENT TIME

REDUCED COST RECOVERY TIME

INCREASED RESPONSIVENESS

MORE SYSTEMATIC APPROACH

TEAM-BASED APPROACH

ITERATIVE APPROACH

DECREASING

* LEAD TIME
* LIFE CYCLE
* BATCH SIZE
* REPEAT ORDERS

2.1 The major trends affecting NPD.

Table 2.1. The number of products being developed at any one time

Number of developments	% of companies
Up to 3	40
4 to 7	30
8 to 11	10
12 and over	20

trends (below) and recognise that the global market is also a global supplier, the true picture emerges.

Some questions to ask

How will you cope with increasing variety?
Because it is the way the world is going you will need to address this issue.

Can you turn this trend to advantage?
By building in service or solving customers' problems.

Can part of the development be 'sub-contracted'?
To suppliers or specialists to save on costs and/or time and produce a better product.

Increasing differentiation

The evidence for this trend is derived from the literature and from our work with our collaborating companies. Companies tend to use similar development techniques and the logical end result of this would be non-differentiated products of similar performance. Product performance differentiation is being achieved by technology usage, but where the Japanese once led, others are now catching up.

Increasingly, service is becoming an important differentiating factor for the future. Another clear need is for companies to create and exploit the so-called 'emotives'. One of the most prominent of these is that of 'Green' product development and this is discussed in more detail at the end of this section. Among the questions worth considering are:

Some questions to ask

What are your key differentiating factors?
Is it the product, the service or something else that you provide? Knowing this will allow you to improve your competitive advantage.

Table 2.2. NPD lead-times

Lead-time (months)	% of companies
Up to 6	22
7 to 12	26
13 to 18	18
19 to 24	17
Over 24	17

Table 2.3. NPD projected life cycles

Life cycle (years)	% of companies
Up to 5	27
5.1 to 10	45
10.1 to 15	10
15.1 to 20	13
Over 20	5

Can 'face-lifts' be used to advantage?

Greater appeal, life cycle extension, etc, all play a part in differentiation and improving performance.

Lead-time reduction

The figures in Table 2.2 show the new product development lead-time from the initial concept to production start-up/market launch. They are from our 1996 survey. They show a relatively even spread with the average figure being approximately 15 months compared to an average lead-time figure of approximately 22 months in our previous survey. This emphasis on the 'speed to market' requirement is a key competitive element.

Some questions to ask

Should you have an internal focus?
Providing greater use of technology, teams and better organisation.
Should you have an external focus?
Through closer links with customers/suppliers and outside experts.
Should you do both?
As your competitors are probably doing both.

Life-cycle reduction

Table 2.3 shows the 'projected' product life cycles for our 1996 survey from the initial launch to market withdrawal. The average life-cycle figure is approximately 8 years, being significantly lower than that found previously (about 12 years). These results provide clear evidence of the pressure on companies in terms of the life of the developed product.

Some questions to ask

Can you extend the current product life cycle?
With minimum effort for maximum impact.

Is life-cycle design an option for you?
If so, you should investigate it.

Is the product reaching the end of its life?
If so then it needs to be replaced.

Reducing batch sizes and repeat orders

These two related trends are a direct result of the global market and its fragmenting, mass customisation nature. Gearing up for batch sizes of one is becoming the norm.

Some questions to ask

Can you develop a 'flexible' family of products?
Develop products that are easily changed or modified.

Is flexible production important?
Through either systems or well-trained, flexible staff.

Introduction of NPD guides or procedures

There is a significant trend toward the introduction and use of NPD guides and/or procedures. These are specific to product development and not introduced to support other company activities. As such, they need to be practical and non-bureaucratic.

Some questions to ask

Do you have a NPD guide or procedure?
If not then you should seriously consider having one, no matter how rudimentary. There is a reasonable correlation between this and success.

The move towards a more agile company

Given the above trends, companies hoping to survive must improve:

- **Responsiveness**: they must become more sentient.
- **Competence**: by achieving more with less.

- **Quickness**: to attain results speedily.
- **Flexibility**: by using available systems in innovative ways.

All this must be done while retaining the requirements of quality, safety, cost, etc. This is the essence of the agile organisation, which is built on the three pillars of:

- **People**: high quality, well educated, fully business aware and well motivated.
- **Organisation**: flexible and involving suppliers/customers (the virtual company).
- **Technology**: in products, their production and the facilitation of actions.

Some questions to ask

What are the key aspects of your company's agility or responsiveness?
This will be a major influence on the future so address it now.

Managing in a more complex environment

Any development of a new product must start in a 'loose' way by encouraging exploration and experimentation but it must proceed to a 'tighter' level of management control towards the end. At the early stage of experimenting, exploring tangential issues is essential and substantial interference from senior management can be devastating to the time, effort and cost schedule. At the end of a project the key issue is task completion. This 'loose' to 'tight' shift of control during a programme has two requirements:

- Line managers able to use both management styles as required.
- Higher managers able to relinquish detailed control at an early stage in the project.

Neither of these attributes is yet universally recognised as essential aspects of new product development management. Until this is the case it will cause major problems to the efficient handling of increasing complexity.

Some questions to ask

Do you understand the requirements of a successful innovation process?
You should have practical and conceptual models of the innovation process.

Are team role preferences used in selecting project teams?
If not, they should be wherever possible.

Fewer development measures

Managing by controlling the new product development process requires many measures and historically these have been:

- **Internal**: return on investment, variances, time schedules, etc.
- **External**: economic data, competitor information, customer attitudes, profit, etc.

In a complex environment, coping with and analysing such an increasing multitude of measures can be counter-productive. It is now recognised that fewer but more critically important measures should be identified and assessed.

Some questions to ask

How do you measure your NPD performance?
Try to ensure that the measures are meaningful and relevant, even if this makes them hard to get at.

Success rates

It is interesting to look at companies' evaluation of success rate (results from the authors' surveys and collaborators and from literature). This is shown in Table 2.4. Only about 10% of all products developed make a significant contribution to sales and profits. Some 30% fail, as defined by the companies.

Table 2.4. NPD success rates

% success of new products	% of companies
Over 75	34
51 to 75	25
26 to 50	29
Up to 25	12

Success measures

In terms of the actual definition of the term 'successful new product', the key company measures now revolve around customer satisfaction and acceptance. These are followed by profitability. There has been a significant shift in the importance placed on quality as a measure of new product success. What is, perhaps, of more interest is the fact that companies found it relatively easy to define success in measurable terms. In earlier studies, companies found it difficult to produce clear measures of success and failure. So performance measures are being better applied.

Some questions to ask

Do the measures you use add value to the company?
If not, change them.

'Green' issues as a key market driver

The 'Green' issues are driven by two independent but related forces, the emergence of global markets and the primacy of the consumer. Concern for all aspects of the environment is now a clear global trend identified by all major long-term forecasting institutes. The 'Green' philosophy has been adopted by all political parties and legislation and the activities of a range of pressure groups are ensuring that this trend will increase significantly. At the same time consumers (in all their guises) are becoming more aware of, and influenced by, environmental issues concerning the development, production and disposal of products. Thus legislation and consumer demands will ensure that 'Green' product development becomes a business factor. Rather than simply responding to these pressures, companies need to learn how to address them as a means of improving competitive advantage and profits.

The concept of environmentally sustainable development was originally proposed by the 'Club of Rome' in the 1970s in which they launched the concept of

'**Factor Four**: Transformation technology that will double wealth whilst halving the use of resources.'

The Environmental Protection Act leads the way in this, with BS 7750 (ISO 14000) providing voluntary guidelines similar to BS 5750 (ISO 9000).

European legislation under EMAS and ISO 14000 are now the control guidelines for European companies. Strategies that companies might adopt in response to legislation fall into three categories:

- Compliance with regulations – a minimum.
- Compliance plus.
- Sustainable development.

This has led to the development of the total quality environmental management (TQEM) concept that allows 'Green' products to be developed within the framework of a TQM system focused on a 'Green' manufacturing system.

Some questions to ask

Are you addressing 'Green' issues for products and their production?
If not then get started as you will have to in the near future and it can be a source of competitive advantage.

Can you use the Factor Four concept when developing products?
Again, a great source of competitive advantage.

2.4 References and indicative reading

'Benchmarking the firm's critical success factors in new product development', R G Cooper and E J Kleinschmidt, *Journal of Product Innovation Management*, **12**: 374–391, November (1995).

Factor Four, E U Weizsacker, A B Lovins and L H Lovins, Earthscan Publications Ltd, London, ISBN 1-85383-407-6 (1989).

Green Design, Dorothy Mackenzie, Calman & King, London, ISBN 1-85669-096-2 (1997).

Ecodesign – A Promising Approach to Sustainable Production and Consumption, Han Brezel and Carolin van Hemel, UNEP/Rathenau Instituit/TU, Delft, ISBN 92-807-1631-X (1997).

European Standard EN ISO 14001.

'Measuring product development success and failure: a framework defining success and failure', E J Hultink and H S J Robben, *The PDMA Handbook of New Product Development*, M D Rosenau (Ed) Wiley, New York, pp. 455–461 (1996).

'Metrics: a practical example', Leland R Beaumont, *The PDMA Handbook of New Product Development*, Wiley, New York, pp. 463–485 (1996).

New Products Management (5th edn), M Crawford, Richard D Irwin, Chicago (1997).

'PDMA success measurement project: recommended measures of development success and failure', Abbie Griffin and Albert Page, *Journal of Product Innovation*

Management, **13**: 478–496 (1996).

Performance Measurement in Service Business, Lin Fitzgerald, Robert Johnson, Stan Brignall, Rhian Silvestro, and Christopher Voss, The Chartered Institute of Management Accountants, London (1991).

Winning at New Products: Accelerating the Process from Idea to Launch, R G Cooper, Second Edition, Addison-Wesley, Reading, MA (1993).

3

Strategic issues in improving NPD performance

3.1 Introduction

This section is included to give an overview of the key strategic issues relating to product development performance. Having a clearly defined NPD strategy is one of the key factors that correlates directly with NPD market success. The practical application of these strategic issues is described in Section 6.

3.2 NPD as a business growth driver

One of the main driving forces in most organisations is the desire for growth. Growth brings with it a positive attitude and enthusiasm for the business, which, in turn, generates the energy needed for future success. Two types of growth exist (as defined by Page and Jones), both related to product development:

- **Internal (or organic) growth**: developing your own products.
- **External growth**: 'buying in' new products.

Internal growth is achieved by internal development and the most important success factors are:

- **Product innovation**: the constant introduction of new and modified products.
- **'Hard' selling**: market focused and sales driven.
- **High profile leadership**: dedicated, high-quality people in key positions.

The key issues may be grouped into the company's product and strategy (Table 3.1).

External growth is regarded as a step-wise process, with 'marriages of consent' being more successful than hostile take-overs. The key factors for this type of growth are:

Table 3.1. The product/strategy issues

Product	Strategy
Desired product	Client focused growth
Good quality	Calculated risk
Hard selling	Planned investment
Product extension	Long term targets
Market led	Day-to-day targets
Market 'wise'	Vertical communication
	A business 'nose'

- **Strategic fit**: one that adds value to both parties.
- **People**: with potential and the retention of key individuals.
- **High autonomy**: managers are encouraged to run the business.
- **Financial control**: tight, within an agreed framework of plans.

Thus products and product development capability are acquired from outside sources.

The focus of this section is directed at achieving the correct balance between internal and external product development that companies need to address.

Some questions to ask

What are your company's main driving forces?
This will influence your NPD approach.

3.3   Defining the influence of the external environment

To give meaningful purpose to the company's new product development activities, it is necessary to be fully aware of the external influences. An external appraisal may be divided into five aspects:

- **Forecasting**: the environment.
- **Strategic framework analysis**: economic, legal, political, etc.
- **Competitive factors**: market and competitive factors.
- **Market framework**: demand and structure.
- **The 'chaos' approach**: managing turbulent and volatile markets.

Forecasting

Producing forecasts is a process of systematically evaluating and developing different views of the future. Forecasting forces you to think about the factors that will affect and influence the new products that you develop. It identifies important changes in the environment and allows you to make appropriate changes. The main techniques are:

- **Extrapolation**: extending current trends.
- **Leading indicator**: does anything vary in line with your activities?
- **Modelling**: encompassing the main factors influencing your company's NPD activities.
- **Scenarios**: creating 'pictures' or 'visions' of the future.
- **Expert opinions**: using the Delphi technique to collect and sort expert opinion.
- **Intuition**: do not be afraid to trust 'gut feeling'. Some companies are building intuition into their NPD programme initiation procedures.

Some questions to ask

Do you have a forecasting 'system'?
You should have, no matter how rudimentary. Simply getting forward projections from key customers is a good start.

Do you review past trends in terms of orders, workload, etc?
This is fairly simple to do and can reduce uncertainty, overloads, etc.

Strategic framework analysis

The factors to be considered in the external appraisal are many, such as the political climate and public opinion. To simplify this, a commonly used approach is the 'STEP' factors analysis:

- **S**ociological: values, lifestyles, demographics, etc.
- **T**echnological: R&D, new products and processes, etc.
- **E**conomic: growth rates, inflation, interest rates, etc.
- **P**olitical: legislation, politics, etc.

Changes in STEP factors can make your competitive position stronger or weaker. The relative importance of each factor will vary from organisation to organisation and from time to time.

Some questions to ask

Do you keep abreast of the non-technical trends?
Simple changes in interest rates or public opinion can have a major impact on activities.

Competitive factors

Michael Porter has defined five 'competitive rivalry' forces, or business threats that impact on a company's competitive capability. These are threats from potential entrants, substitutes, buyer power, suppliers and general competitive rivalry.

- **Potential entrants**: entrants increase competition and the main barriers to entry are technology, costs, economics, product differentiation and customer loyalty. Low entry barriers lead to easy entrance and market fragmentation. Existing companies should try to erect high entry barriers via their product developments.
- **Substitutes**: can alternative products or materials perform the same function but with competitive advantage (lower cost, better quality, etc.)? Emergence of substitutes increases the buyer's power. This is a difficult area to identify early enough to take action.
- **Buyer power**: the dangers here are when purchases are a significant proportion of the buyer's cost; when purchases are undifferentiated and when the buyer's profits are low.
- **Supplier power**: is detrimental in a market with few suppliers or substitutes, especially supplying differentiated products. This power also increases if the industry supplied is not an important customer or the product is important to the buyer.
- **Competitive rivalry**: the actual basis for competitive rivalry can take many forms from price to after-sales service. The number of competitors, the growth rate, costs, profits, capacity, diversification, etc, all influence this.

Each industrial sector is shaped by these five factors and each company will be individually placed within it. Once the company's place within the industry is understood, the strategic factors will be far more easily analysed in terms of improving product development performance.

Some questions to ask

Can you move into less competitive markets?
Admittedly difficult to do but well worth trying.

Can you gain competitive advantage by means other than technical expertise?
Among the strategies here are solving the customers' problems, offering both a product and a service, etc.

A market framework

A distinct market may be said to exist if there are no 'close' substitutes for a product or service, i.e. the product or service is differentiated from that of its competitors. Differentiation means that your product or service is 'different' from that of your competitors. The difference may be real or it may be perceived. If the market is made up of products that are relatively similar, then the price and service competition will be fierce. The key factors in the market framework are as follows:

- **Demand**: its size and pattern. What is the total demand and its trend? What divisions and segments are there within the market? How mature is the product or market?
- **Product life cycle**: new products are developed and are then replaced by other products that begin, catch on, mature and then fall away. In simple terms, this is the product life cycle. In the early part of the cycle there is little competition, whereas in the mature, declining part, there is intense competition.
- **Costs**: their scale and pattern. What is the total unit cost of the product or service and the distribution between fixed and variable costs? Are economies of scale important? What about efficiency, learning, excess capacity, etc?

Some questions to ask

Are you constantly trying to reduce costs?
This is a must for most companies.

Are there other options than constant cost cutting?
What 'value' can be added to your products to make them more attractive, e.g. facelifts, service extension.

The 'chaos' approach

The new competitive environment is one of increasing complexity and diversity; one where constant change is the order of the day. Recently, the work on chaos theory (see Stacey) has been equated to this turbulent environment, especially as to how companies 'organise' themselves to deal with the chaotic environment by becoming more flexible, agile and responsive. The three keys are:

- **People**: well trained, educated and motivated with a good business awareness that allows them to take decisions quickly.

- **Organisation**: flexible and fluid with senior managers in facilitating and supporting roles rather than directing and controlling.
- **Technology**: that enables people to do their job better.

One large and very successful company (J C Bamford Ltd) has a routine that is applied to all people. It is this:

'What is your job? ... How can you do it better? ... How can you do it faster?'

In essence, this is what the improvement of NPD performance is about in both strategic and immediate terms.

Some questions to ask

Can you and your staff summarise the company's key values (as J C Bamford)?
It appears to be a simple task, but try doing it. It is difficult but worthwhile.

3.4   Defining strategic options

Various options are available to address product development strategy and these approaches need to be reviewed as a means of taking advantage of future opportunities and countering possible threats. These options may be categorised into two broad approaches:

- **Reactive NPD strategies**: deal with pressures as they occur (such as copying a successful product of a competitor).
- **Proactive NPD strategies**: identify and capture opportunities and try to be first in the market-place.

Either strategic approach to product development is appropriate under certain conditions and the company must recognise the need for change and prepare accordingly (organisationally, technologically, etc.). The adoption of any one strategic option brings with it its own series of questions to be addressed.

Reactive NPD strategies

- **Defensive**: makes changes in existing products to counteract a competitor's successful launch. At its most aggressive, the company can strike pre-emptively at a projected new product launch with a marketing campaign.

- **Imitative**: quick copying or a 'me too' policy. On a national basis this was Japan in the 1950s. A good example is the fashion industry copying the fashion houses.
- **Second but better**: similar to Imitative but produces an improved copy. Flexibility and efficiency are needed.
- **Response**: purposefully reacting to customer's requests. Scientific instruments are a good example of this.

Proactive NPD strategies

- **Research & development**: investment in the future-oriented R&D effort.
- **Marketing**: finding a consumer need and then producing a product to fill it.
- **Entrepreneurial**: an individual makes an idea happen through a venture. How many 'high-tech' companies in 'Silicon Valley' started.
- **Acquisition**: firms purchase companies with new technology, products or markets.

Reactive strategies demand short lead-time to copy, low entry cost and unprotected innovation. The balance between reactive and proactive strategy is shown in Table 3.2.

With a proactive NPD strategy, a company must control risk and at the same time encourage creative development. The basic problem is that organisations tend to nullify creative endeavour. Managers must develop an organisation that is disciplined and yet creative. This can be done but requires fully trained and business-aware people at all levels, with clear objectives and top level support.

Table 3.2. Balancing NPD strategies

Reactive strategy	Proactive strategy
Concentrate on existing products	Desire growth in new products and markets
Little innovation protection	Patenting or achieve market penetration
Small markets, intense competition	High-volume/high-margin markets
	Resources available restrict competition

Some questions to ask

If you have a mixture of strategies, is the balance right?
Most companies do have a mixture (by necessity) and keeping the balance right is difficult to do but essential.

If you have a single strategic option, is it viable in the long term?
Using a single option demands a great deal of commitment. Check that what you are doing is sustainable, as far as can be seen, in the long term.

3.5 Defining the strategic focus

Having conducted the appropriate external review and considered the strategic options, the next part of the product development strategy review is to determine the focus of the strategy: how the strategic aims will be met in practice.

- **Internal development**: this is the development option relying on the skills, capabilities and competencies within the company. If they do not already exist to meet defined opportunities, then they must be developed or brought in.
- **'Buying' a way into the business**: the routes here are essentially all external, including acquisition, joint ventures or partnerships and, less common in product development terms, turn around.
- **Focusing on a specific product**: if you are dealing with a specific product development, then you can focus on it and devote appropriate resources to its development.
- **Dealing with a range of products**: if this is the case, then a more comprehensive programme of work is needed, especially when reviewing the integrating activities and the development process.

The options are shown in Fig. 3.1, which is based on the Ansoff matrix (see below).

Some questions to ask

Do you have a single focus?
Beware of the 'not invented here' syndrome. Fast routes to market can be gained by product acquisition.

Can you diversify?
Either by acquisition or multi product internal development.

To try to help the practical realisation of your strategic review and analysis, optional routes are provided through the flowchart in Appendix 4.

One of the most popular approaches, but by no means the only one, is

	Internal option	*External options*
Product specific	Review internal capabilities, competencies and resources.	Identify and 'buy in' the appropriate product.
Generic/ overall	Conduct a complete review of your NPD capability.	Identify and 'acquire' the appropriate company.

3.1 The NPD strategic options review.

the use of conceptual models of the business. Such models allow for ease of understanding of the company's business position, especially in relation to that of its competitors. It is worth examining two of the more popular models; there are many more but these two are the most useful for NPD purposes.

The Boston Consultant Group (BCG) matrix

This can be equally applied to products as to businesses and categorises products according to growth rate and market share. It shows which products should be nurtured, 'milked' or left to themselves. This is shown diagrammatically in Fig. 3.2.

- **Stars**: high growth and market penetration; use product development and product extension to maintain advantage.
- **Question marks**: product development work is questionable.
- **Cash cows**: cost reductions and aesthetic improvements.
- **Dogs**: ripe for deletion.

The BCG matrix position is closely linked with another concept, that of the experience curve. This states that the overall unit costs of making a

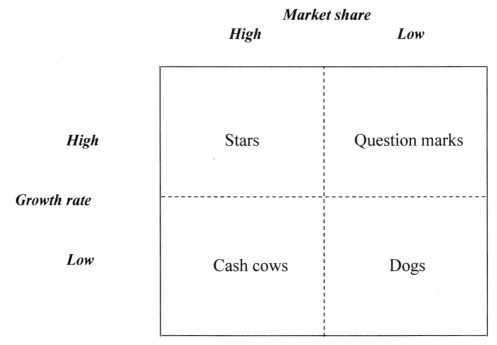

3.2 The Boston Consulting Group (BCG) matrix.

product decline with experience (some 30% each time the production unit output is doubled).

The market/product matrix (Ansoff)

This is useful in differentiating between market or product-oriented development (Fig. 3.3). The choice of which strategy to adopt depends largely on the company's reaction to several influencing factors. Growth opportunities may come from any one of the cells in the matrix.

- **Activity in Cell 1**: implies that the company is good at production and distribution and growth rate plans are not high. A reactive strategy is appropriate.
- **Activity in Cell 2**: arises because of market saturation. Companies seek new uses for existing products.
- **Activity in Cell 3**: the most common kind of growth strategy, i.e. attacking existing markets with new products; 'building on our strengths'.

Product

	Existing	New
Existing	1. Market penetration	3. Product development
New	2. Market development	4. Diversification

Market

3.3 The Ansoff matrix.

- **Activity in Cell 4**: implies diversification in both product and market.

To operate in Cells 2, 3 and 4, companies mainly use a proactive strategy based on an innovative growth process, on sound R & D and marketing expertise.

Some questions to ask

Do you review your current product portfolio regularly?
It is important to do this as all products die (or are killed).

Do you 'dispose' of the unprofitable products?
This should be done cautiously as they may still contribute to overhead costs.

Do you project forward your developments in the light of the portfolio review?
This is essential in order to avoid product 'gaps' and resultant loss of income.

Are you looking for new markets?
The Ansoff matrix is useful here. For example, trying to find new markets for ageing products sometimes can be extremely rewarding.

3.6   References and indicative reading

Strategic Thinking and the Management of Change – International Perspectives on Organisational Dynamics, Ralph Stacey, Kogan Page, London (1993).

Managing Chaos: Dynamic Business Strategies in an Unpredictable World, Ralph Stacey, Kogan Page, London (1992).

The Chaos Frontier, Creative Strategic Control of Businesses, Ralph Stacey, 1991.

Business Growth – How to Achieve and Sustain It, A S Page and R C Jones, MCB Press, Bradford (1989).

In Search of Excellence, T J Peters and R H Waterman, Harper & Row, New York (1982).

Understanding Organisations, C B Handy, Penguin Books, London, pp. 177–85 (1981).

Competitive Strategy – Techniques for Analysing Industries and Competitors, M E Porter, The Free Press, New York (1980).

The Structuring of Organisations, H Mintzberg, Prentice-Hall, Englewood Cliffs, NJ (1979).

Strategy and Structure, A D Chandler, MIT, Boston, MA (1962).

Leadership and Organisation Development Journal, **10**, No. 2, MCB Press, Bradford.

4

Evaluating product development performance

4.1 Introduction

In order to increase NPD success rates, an increasing number of companies are adopting a systematic approach to evaluating the success of developments and then interpreting their findings to drive a continuous process of improvement. However, in the current turbulent competitive environment it is not sufficient simply to carry out a retrospective analysis of how a product has performed once it has reached the market-place. Rather, because performance in the development process has a significant effect upon the commercial success of the product development, performance needs to be measured regularly from the start of a programme and continued until well after product launch. Comparing the actual results or outcomes with goals and targets helps identify areas of excellence and weakness that can be used to set the agenda for improvement.

The main problems for practitioners lie in deciding what is to be measured and then extracting meaningful lessons from the results to direct the improvement process. This chapter discusses the relative merits of performance metrics associated with the evaluation of product development performance and identifies difficulties and solutions to the development of performance measurement systems.

4.2 Product development success and failure

Distinguishing between product success and failure is not always easy because a product may be successful in one area yet fail in another. The paradox of the product that succeeds technically but does not perform in the market is a problem often encountered by companies and is difficult to decipher. Without technical success, business success is unobtainable but technical achievement does not necessarily guarantee a commercial triumph. Furthermore, the likelihood of market failure increases the longer products are in development, particularly in fast-moving, competitive markets. Protracted or delayed product development can cause companies to lose sales as customer expectations shift over time or competitors beat them to the market-place. Development costs also rise as more resources are used. These effects impact on the financial performance of the programme.

If a company wishes to achieve NPD success, it not only needs to evaluate success in multiple dimensions, it will also need to do so throughout the product's life cycle, from its conception through to decline. The successful product will be one that performs well in all categories. These are a rare commodity, as requirements often have to be traded off against each other.

4.3   Product development performance metrics

Only recently has there been a widespread understanding of the need to measure the different facets of success using product development performance metrics. A number of studies have attempted to define and categorise them. One of the most recent and extensive surveys carried out in the US reviewed the research in product development performance over the past ten years and identified over 75 distinct performance measures (Griffin). Sixteen core measures were extracted as being of use by practitioners. These fall into two broad bands or levels of performance metrics:

- **Firm level**: these are used to measure the overall performance of the product development activity within the company or a particular strategic business unit within a corporation.
- **Programme level**: these relate to the performance of individual products, the efficiency of their development and market-place performance.

Firm level metrics

A number of metrics exist at the firm level to establish the overall success rate of development programmes. They are as follows:

- Development programme return on investment.
- New products that fit business strategy.
- Success/failure rate.
- Percentage profit from new products (newer than three years old, say).
- Percentage sales from new products.
- Products that lead to future opportunities.

One of the most common measures of the performance of product development programmes at the firm level is the percentage of sales revenue spent on R&D. This is rather misleading as spending more is equated with better. Studies have shown little correlation between the level of spending and success. The R&D Effectiveness Index (EI) (McGrath) sets out to remedy this problem by comparing profit from new products to the investment in new product development. The EI calculates the ratio of new products relative to the investment in product development:

$$EI = \frac{\%\ new\ product\ revenue \times \left(net\ profit\ \% + R\&D\ \%\right)}{R\&D\ \%}$$

(% are relative to revenue)

When the ratio is greater than 1.0, the return from new product is greater than that invested. Initial studies show that there is a reasonable correlation between this and revenue growth (McGrath).

Programme level metrics

A useful way to look at the different types of product development performance metrics at the programme level is to differentiate between those that are determined within the organisation (internal efficiency) and those that are used once the product is in the market (external effectiveness). This is shown diagrammatically in Fig. 4.1.

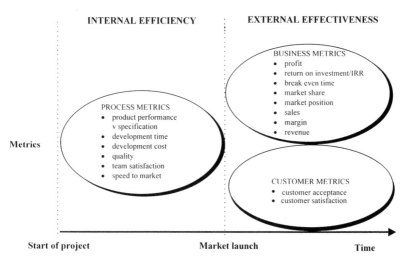

4.1 Balancing NPD performance metrics (IRR = internal rate of return).

Internal efficiency

The internal efficiency metrics relate directly to the performance of the product development process and are usually the easiest to understand and measure. The danger can be that too much emphasis is placed on measuring them to the detriment of external effectiveness. These measures can be recorded regularly throughout the development process and used to gauge the actions required to move actual development performance in line with targets. Our UK surveys support evidence from a survey carried out with Dutch firms that measuring performance against specification is the chief measure to evaluate during the development process alongside meeting quality standards.

Development cost is cited as being one of the most important metrics that should be in place. This is not simply budgeting but also a record of the intensity at which the programme funds are spent.

External effectiveness

In the case of the external efficiency metrics, the business measures of profit, pay back and rates of return are usually addressed by systems that are already in place. The return map can be a useful way of illustrating programme finances (Fig. 4.2).

Of the external-based measures, it is the customer-based measures that present the most difficulty. Simply relying on the business measures as a means of reflecting customer satisfaction is no longer acceptable. The new operating environment requires specific measures of customer acceptance and satisfaction and it will be these that will have the most influence on businesses in the future.

Customer satisfaction has become the key indicator of product develop-

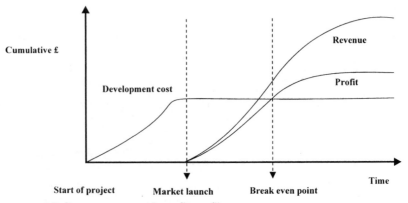

4.2 Programme cost/benefit profile.

ment performance emphasising the need for customer-focused businesses. Common metrics used are number of returned products or customer complaints. However, these measures show extreme cases of dissatisfaction and do not indicate the perceptions of customers who are moderately or extremely satisfied with their purchase and have a valid input to improving the product. Surveys, interviews and focus groups using the views not just of consumers but of dealers and the sales force are the chief means of gleaning this information.

It is important not to ask customers simply to measure the performance of the physical product against their expectations but to evaluate intangible aspects of the product such as style, prestige, feel and aesthetic appearance, which also influence their perception. Companies should also consider measuring the 'service' elements of the product, which are critical to customer satisfaction. These could include any of the following: reliability, responsiveness, cleanliness and tidiness, comfort, friendliness, communication, courtesy, competence, access, availability, security.

Some questions to ask

Do you know how successful your products are?
Evaluating the success of a development is a vital part of directing the improvement process.

Do you evaluate the overall performance of your development activity?
This is a good indication of the health of the company and a useful means of comparison with the competition.

Do you use internal and external metrics?
It is important that both are used in the context of NPD and that the latter is not viewed simply as a general business measure.

Do you set performance goals and targets?
These will give your development programmes focus and measurable outputs to drive team members.

Can you relate internal and external success?
This is extremely difficult to do. But a good internal performance is more likely to lead to a good external result.

4.4 Measuring the quality of the development process

Extending beyond the view of outcomes of the development process, whether that be on the firm or programme level, there has been increasing interest in developing means of measuring the quality of processes or practices involved in developing the products. These present themselves in the form of benchmarking or audit tools and promote the use of best practice in product development.

Cooper has developed a benchmarking tool, which is aimed at identifying the firm's critical success factors in NPD. It uses two sets of measures:

- Programme profitability: market-place based.
- Programme impact: the effect on the company's internal environment.

It links them to the quality of performance of the product development practices. The survey reveals that success was achieved where there was a high-quality new product process, a clear, well-communicated new product strategy for the company, adequate resources for new products, senior management commitment to new products and an entrepreneurial climate for product innovation.

In the broader context of innovation management London Business School has developed an innovation audit process model of technical innovation based on managerial, processes and organisational mechanisms. Four 'core processes' are identified: concept generation, product development, process innovation and technology acquisition.

While these systems are useful, they all have the problem that they are based on retrospective analysis. One of the few tools for performance measurement that has a major forward view element is the Readiness Assessment for Concurrent Engineering (RACE) tool developed by the Concurrent Engineering Research Centre in West Virginia, USA. The problem here is that it applies only to very large corporations (mainly in the defence industry) and is extremely difficult to use.

The assessment tool and methodology (ATM)

The ATM examines the performance of the development process and of the activities which assist the integration of people, process and information for the development of products. Its practical application is described in Part III.

Some questions to ask

What have you done to improve the NPD environment?
Try to determine how it has changed over the past years.

Do you know how good your NPD process is?
Compare it to those of other companies, especially companies with best practice.

4.5   Developing a performance measurement system

Given that there are a wide range of performance metrics, being able to apply the relevant ones becomes the next issue. Performance measurement systems have developed in tandem with the introduction and use of formal NPD procedures. At a base level, these tend to be project management systems, usually based on a computer package. The problem with these is that their primary objectives are to organise, plan and manage the progress of the project or programme. The metrics that are used in these systems are those that the system provides, which are not necessarily those that are wanted or needed. As with the development of NPD procedures, it is essential that the measurement system used be tailored to the company's needs. This means that it has to be developed by the company itself.

The best way to do this is first to define the performance metrics that are essential to the company. The relative importance of the measures depends on the peculiarities of the product in question. In particular, the 'newness' of the product reflects the appropriateness of measures. At the market level, customer satisfaction and acceptance are generally important but market share is most important for 'new to the company' products (Fig. 4.3).

At the programme level, the metrics used tend to relate to the company's innovation strategy. A low-innovation business strategy leads to more concern with efficiency while a high-innovation business strategy leads to more concern regarding the impact on company growth.

Once these are known, then a system can be produced that provides them. Often this is a mixture of commercially available project management software and 'home-grown' systems. Product development is about managing the present to provide for the future, thus there needs to be a balance between what is happening now and what is needed to happen in the future.

'Let's measure what we need to know and not what we can'

We now know what we need to measure, why and how important it is to the company. All that remains is to ensure that we have a performance measurement system that will produce the required information. The first step here is to determine how each metric is to be produced. Some will be easy and probably already in existence. Others will be much more difficult but once included at this stage, means of defining them must be found. Until this is done, an effective system cannot be produced so spend time at this stage to find the most cost-effective method(s) to use.

The final step is to develop/modify a system that gives you the maximum

	Newness to the Market	
New to the Company • Market share • Revenue or satisfaction • Meet profit goal • Competitive advantage		**New to the World** • Customer acceptance • Customer satisfaction • Meet profit goal or IRR/ROI • Competitive advantage
Product Improvements • Customer satisfaction • Market or revenue growth • Meet profit goal • Competitive advantage	**Additions to Existing Lines** • Market share • Revenue growth Customer satisfaction and acceptance • Meet profit goal • Competitive advantage	
Cost Reductions • Customer satisfaction • Acceptance or revenue • Meet margin goal • Performance or quality	**Product Repositioning** • Customer acceptance • Satisfaction or share • Meet profit goal • Competitive advantage	

(Vertical axis: **Newness to the Company**)

4.3 Balance of newness and market performance measures (ROI = return on investment).

amount of information for the minimum effort. Having clearly defined what it is that you need, you can be reasonably sure that time and effort put into accessing the metrics will not be wasted.

Most systems appear to be a blend of current systems that exist for other functions (e.g. project networks, management information systems, etc) and dedicated NPD systems. Make use of anything that already exists and develop that that does not. Try to integrate them into a system that has the minimum level of bureaucracy. The most significant factor that multi-national Japanese companies all have in common is the lack of bureaucracy in their systems. Performance metrics and targets are clearly defined and understood; after this their philosophy is 'we talk to each other'.

Some questions to ask

Do you have an efficient and effective performance measurement system?

This should be a system dedicated to the NPD activities and process and not a simple extension of other business measurement systems.

4.6   The future of performance measurement

There is no doubt that measuring product development performance has become, and will remain, an important issue for most companies. This progression has occurred since the 1980s and is shown in Fig. 4.4.

Most companies are now through the quality systems 'barrier' and are looking toward product development and agility as the next drivers for growth. The degree of importance and the focus will vary between companies and even between different products within the same company. The important aspect about the above diagram is that as one moves from bottom left to top right, the move is from certainty and stability to uncertainty and turbulence.

This is the new operational environment, and product development activities and process need to reflect this. At the heart of this are the changes needed in the performance measurement metrics and systems that are used. The days have now gone where cost and quality could be used as the main indicators for performance. The advent of mass customisation and the increasing importance of service and responsiveness (agility) reflect the rise of the importance of the consumer, whether that consumer is a single person or another company.

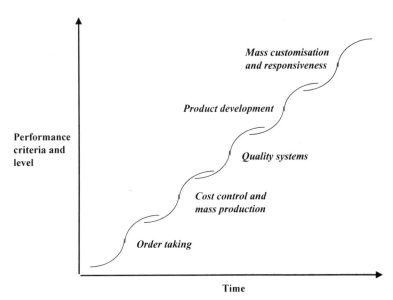

4.4 Performance measurement trends.

Companies need NPD performance metrics and measurement systems that reflect the new environment and thus allow them to prosper in an increasingly turbulent operating environment.

4.7   References and indicative reading

'PDMA success measurement project: recommended measures of development success and failure', Abbie Griffin and Albert Page, *Journal of Product Innovation Management*, **13**: 478–496 (1996).

'Measuring new product success: the difference that the time perspective makes', Erik Hutlink and Henry Robben, *Journal of Product Innovation Management*, **12**: 392–405 (1995).

'Measuring development performance in the electronics industry', Christoph Loch, Lothar Stein and Christian Terwiesch, *Journal of Product Innovation Management*, **13**: 3–20 (1996).

'Metrics: a practical example', Leland R Beaumont, *The PDMA Handbook of New Product Development*, Wiley, New York, pp. 463–485 (1996).

'Measuring product development success and failure: a framework defining success and failure', E J Hultink and H S J Robben, *The PDMA Handbook of New Product Development*, Wiley, New York, pp. 455–461 (1996).

Performance Measurement in Service Business, Lin Fitzgerald, Robert Johnson, Stan Brignall, Rhian Silvestro and Christopher Voss, The Chartered Institute of Management Accountants, London (1991).

'Developing products and services: how do you know how well you've done?', Abbie Griffin, Presentation at the 2nd Annual Program of Improving Product Development: Lessons from Experts, Houston, TX (1995).

'The R&D Effectiveness Index: a metric for product development', Michael E McGrath and Michael N Romeri, *Journal of Product Innovation Management*, **11**: 213–220 (1994).

'Development of a technical innovation audit', Vittorio Chiesa, Paul, Coughlan and Chris A Voss, *Journal of Product Innovation Management*, **13**: 105–136 (1996).

'Benchmarking the firm's critical success factors in new product development', R G Cooper and E J Kleinschmidt, *Journal of Product Innovation Management*, **12**: 374–391, November (1995).

'Benchmarking firms' new product performance & practices', R G Cooper and E J Kleinschmidt, *Engineering Management Review*, Fall (1995).

Measure Up! The Essential Guide to Measuring Business Performance (2nd edn), Richard L Lynch and Kevin F Cross Mandarin, London (1992).

5

Improving product
development performance

5.1 Introduction

The need to improve, consistently and continuously, all aspects of
a company's performance is well understood. Product development
is no different from any other business process in this respect.
However there are specific problems, the first of which is that the
detailed attention demanded by NPD has only recently emerged as
a key issue. There is also no detailed history of NPD improvement
methods and techniques. NPD outputs are both short term (internal)
and long term (external) and it is probably this last point that causes
most difficulty for organisations. The balance of these is shown in
Fig. 5.1.

- **Sector I**: companies in this sector are operating in markets that are
  dynamic and constantly changing. NPD activities and process have to
  reflect this and they tend to be 'action'-based within their overall strategic framework.
- **Sector II**: development lead times can be significantly longer than the
  market-based time scales. Internal efficiency is paramount, together
  with constant market testing and analysis.
- **Sector III**: we are dealing with long lead-times in both development
  and market impact terms. The key activities here are clear strategy,
  long-term focus (forecasting, etc.) and risk containment and
  management/adjustment.
- **Sector IV**: operating in this sector implies that development lead-times
  are short but market feedback is much longer. Emphasis here must be
  on choosing the correct development.

The above discussion is really at the heart of the improvement of NPD
performance.

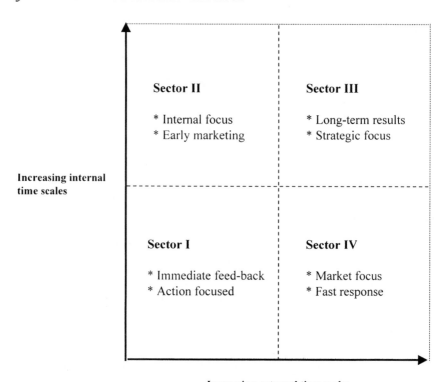

Increasing internal
time scales

Increasing external time scales

5.1 The implications of external and internal time scales.

Some questions to ask

Can you place your products or company into a sector of the matrix?
If you can then check that any improvement work is focused correctly.

5.2   The basic choices

There are two basic approaches to improving NPD performance, and these are:

- **Refinement change**: product development is treated as a business process and is continuously reviewed and refined.
- **Radical change**: a major shift in NPD activities and process usually prompted by poor results or a shift in strategy and/or market.

Refinement change should be the aim, especially if current performance is acceptable. Refinement offers a low-risk strategy and, more importantly, demands that the people involved in the NPD activities and process are involved in the detail. This tends to raise morale and commitment.

Radical change appears to involve a high-risk strategy to rescue a poorly performing system or to make a major change in direction. Although there is no reason why the actual practitioners should not be involved in this type of change, invariably it is top-down driven.

Some questions to ask

Do you recognise the basic requirements of the two approaches?
Refinement change is the general order of the day. It is the process of continuous improvement. Radical change often relates to serious problems though it can also be used to seize unusual opportunities.

5.3   Performance improvement methods

As with the subject of performance metrics, the evidence in this area may be divided into both firm and programme level approaches. Firm level approaches focus on both programme management and the technical/design-build process. An interesting finding is the confirmation of product complexity level as a major determinant of team need. Another general, and novel, approach is that of 'knowledge amplification' as used by Sony and described by Numata. The process of linking essential NPD innovation activities and business performance measures in both theoretical and practical ways still remains the 'Holy Grail'.

Specific NPD performance improvement methods include the long-debated and 'thorny' issue of R&D/marketing integration. Other well-tested improvement methods include:

- The use of cross-functional teamwork.
- R&D's contribution to short- and long-term business results.
- Reducing development lead-times.
- Efficient use of R&D resources.

Specific improvement approaches tend to be of limited practical application while the reported general ones again all tend to rely on retrospective analysis. Examples of performance improvement methods that have had a significant effect on the authors' collaborating companies (see the case studies in Part IV) are:

- **Total co-location**: this has been introduced by several companies to try to overcome the problem of interfacing sales/marketing with the technical function.

- **Structured systems and information support**: this approach has been adopted by BBA Friction Ltd as a means of improving development performance within a strategic framework.
- **Formal assessment procedures and proposal evaluation**: Lantor (UK) Ltd had the problem that it had literally hundreds of potential development programmes and faced extreme difficulty in choosing between them. They overcame this by introducing a formal assessment procedure and proposal evaluation system covering programme, business and market considerations and measures.
- **Introduction of commercial appraisal into NPD process**: Try & Lilly Ltd has intensified the commercial part of their NPD process to support its strategic viewpoint.
- **Post-development audit and review**: J C Bamford Excavators Ltd has introduced post-development assessment and has achieved some impressive results with its use.
- **Structured idea generation and processing**: Continental Sports Ltd has introduced such a system to generate and manage new product ideas. Since its introduction, 41 new product ideas have been generated. Of these, six were taken forward; four were 'killed' at various stages and two emerged into the market. Early indications are that these are quite successful.

Some questions to ask

Can you see any use for any of the above improvement methods?
It is worth trying some (or all). As a starting point we suggest post-development audit and review.

5.4   The integrating activities

The NPD environment encompasses many activities, all of which are needed to allow a development to come to fruition. The model (Appendix 1) presented here was developed to try to reflect the major activities the authors found derived from their varied experience and practical research and from detailed reviews of literature. A common theme of these is that they have some form of 'integrating' effect on the NPD environment, hence our term 'integrating activities'.

What is clear is that different types of industries and/or product developments have differing needs for the use of these integrating activities. Indeed, for some companies the full range may well not be needed (it is mainly the computer-based tools and the formal methods that are not needed). The improvement focus and/or use of each of the activities are discussed below.

People

Cross-functional teams

The use of teams and teamwork is at the heart of integrated product development. In a small company, this may well be the full management team, while in a larger one dedicated programme teams may be set up. Ideally, they should be single status, include all interested functions and be trained in teamwork.

Team leadership

As teamwork is now the norm, team leadership becomes a critical activity. Empowering team members to make decisions without then losing overall control requires a fine balance of knowledge and skills.

Team development

Team members should understand the various roles that have to be in place for successful team effort and the group maintenance activity that is essential for cohesiveness. They should be encouraged to learn new skills and update existing ones. Some measure of multi-skilling is usually useful.

Reward and recognition

Traditional reward systems are no longer compatible with team-based organisations. New methods of reward and recognition need to be introduced, usually focused on the job content motivators rather than job context issues.

Co-location

This is not a pre-requisite for good development performance. However, it is one of the most effective ways of integrating activities and overcoming barriers.

Process

Project management

This allows for greater control over the NPD progression and creates a sense of wholeness. Direct reporting to top management usually means that issues are dealt with speedily.

Formal NPD procedures

This is an area that has gained rapidly in popularity. They provide a degree of consistency and reduce variability in the development process. They should be specifically designed to support the development process and not as a 'tag-on' to quality system procedures.

Customer/supplier integration

Customers and suppliers should be involved in the development process at the earliest moment. Indeed, suppliers form a good source of development activity themselves.

Formal team briefings

These are essential for the dissemination of information and the discussion of current status.

Organisational re-design

This entails establishing suitable organisational forms to support the development of new products. This includes the use of matrix structures or dedicated programme teams but is now being extended into the 'virtual' organisation where team members are brought together through the use of information technology (IT) systems while being geographically separated.

Computer-based tools

Computers/networks

These are used to integrate departmental functions and provide a common database of up-to-date product information. They also provide a means of communicating information both locally and remotely.

Computer-aided design (CAD)

The rapid development of design models using approaches such as surface and solid modelling. Output can also be used directly for other purposes (computer-aided modelling, rapid prototyping, etc.).

Computer-aided engineering (CAE)

CAE involves the use of analytical software such as finite element analysis for testing and evaluating designs.

Simulation

Software is used to simulate the operation of components or the manufacturing process.

Formal methods

Quality function deployment (QFD)

A structured method is used to incorporate customer requirements, especially the intangibles into the design process. It helps companies to develop products around real market needs as opposed to what they think is needed.

Design of experiments (DoE)

Statistical methods are used to converge on optimum solutions for testing products by testing selected parameters (e.g. Taguchi). This helps to produce products that work well in a wide range of conditions. DoE methods are used extensively in process related industries.

Design for manufacture (DFM)

Companies should consider manufacturing implications in their design. DFM is another quantitative method that may be used to analyse designs and ensure that manufacture works well and at minimum cost.

Failure mode and effects analysis (FMEA)

FMEA is used to indicate priority in failure of products or parts. Failure is determined by severity, frequency and detectability of potential faults.

Some questions to ask

Which aspects of the above does your development environment use?

The computer-based tools and the formal methods are much more common for engineering companies and for those companies operating in difficult to define markets.

Where do you see improvements may be made?

In our experience it is the people issues that cause companies the most difficulties.

5.5   The product development process

In line with the model of the development environment described above, two models of the development process are recommended:

- **13-step process**: this is a stepwise process based on the published research and practical evidence. It is useful in terms of understanding the steps that might be used (though not all companies will use them all) and the influence of the process entry point. This model is shown in Appendix 2.
- **Stage gate process**: this is more of a control model to be used once the overall process has been defined. The stage gates are the points at which 'go' or 'no-go' decisions are made. This model is shown in Fig. 5.2.

The 13-step process

The 13-step process model is shown in Appendix 2 and is a stepwise process as follows.

Step 1. Initial screening

Most firms use some form of screening criteria for new products. However, the activity ranges from ad hoc to 'overly formal', and difficulties lie with finding the right balance between the two. The main difficulty is in saying 'no' to projects. This is particularly a problem where firms have little resource to spend on new products, and so resource tends to be diluted unnecessarily.

Step 2. Preliminary market assessment

Unlike detailed marketing studies, preliminary market assessments are based on 'feeling the ground' for new products (e.g. assessing volumes, and monitoring competitor activity in the area). However, the criticality of this activity varies significantly across firms. For example, where much of a firm's business comes from direct enquiries from customers, then the activity is less critical than for those firms that supply their goods direct to market. In this latter case, several of our firms expressed the view that more formality is needed because often information is not accurate and, on occasions, information is missing altogether.

Step 3. Preliminary technical assessment

All our collaborating companies understood this activity to be vital, and high levels of criticality tended to be matched by high levels of perceived proficiency. Both the level of risk involved in new programmes and the degree of 'newness' of products have a significant bearing on this variable. For example, one firm, which operates in a niche market whereby innovations are relatively rare, perceived the activity to be of 'low' criticality. Alternatively, another firm that develops fashion-type goods to a risky market rated the activity as 'highly' critical. As one manager suggested, 'it comes down to money. If you are going to spend a lot of money on the project, then it makes sense to do a thorough assessment'.

Step 4. Detailed marketing assessment

Many firms recognised the criticality of detailed marketing studies. In practice, however, few firms engage in the activity and the most often-cited reason for its absence involved the lack of resource availability. Variables that affect the criticality of the activity include being in an established or niche market, the level of newness of the product, and the confidence the firm feels at being in new markets. Most firms see this as a major area for improvement, especially those firms that are breaking out into new markets (e.g. ex-defence contractors) and that have little or no experience of the changing demands of commercial markets.

Step 5. Pre-development business analysis

Rather than being a discrete NPD task, assessing the viability of new product programmes is considered by many managers to be an ongoing task. Experience suggests that this activity is carried out reasonably well. The main constraint posed to adequate analyses at this stage is the lack of good quality marketing data (Step 4).

Step 6. Product development

The product development phase is among the most critical of all activities, especially among engineering-based firms. The more technical and less familiar the product and the newer the market, then the greater the need to invest in prototypes. Significant criticisms involved the timing element, co-ordination among the different functions, and the changing/evolving nature of product specifications. In contrast, the criticality of product development for process-oriented firms is less, and in instances where designs were relatively mature, then the activity is almost non-existent.

Step 7. In-house product testing

Most firms have significant experience with product testing, and do not perceive the activity to be in need of improvement. The level of product testing tended to vary based on the complexity of the design, the location of the product in the overall structure of the assembly, and finally volumes. In the latter instance, where first products are prototypes, then working closely with customers is critical because of the time delay. Doing meaningful in-house trials would delay the launch date, and the costs would be excessive, so there is a corresponding need to test new products 'live' with customers.

Step 8. Customer testing of the product

Variables that appear to affect the level of activity concerning customer tests are the origin of the specification, the volume of new products produced, and the relative costs of failure. Where new products are developed against an internally generated specification, then the more likely it is that customers will be given samples or actual products to test.

Step 9. Test marketing and trial selling

Test marketing and trial selling of new products is seen to have only limited usefulness to most firms, especially where this relates to assessing the potential uptake for new products. However, in several cases firms did suggest they had recently given a customer a product to assess, owing mainly to the level of 'newness' of the product being developed.

Step 10. Trial production

For engineering firms in particular, trial production is often seen to be an activity in need of improvement. The most important variable suggested to affect the criticality of the activity concerned the potential volume of new products (i.e. the higher the volume of products produced, the more critical the activity). For the process industries the activity is critical.

Step 11. Pre-commercial analysis

Several of the collaborating companies' managers suggested that this task is too late in the NPD cycle, and because marketing assessments are lacking, then it is very difficult to carry out the task properly. Where the activity does occur, information was suggested to be too fragmented.

Step 12. Production start-up

While this activity was perceived to be of high importance, the perceived proficiency or conduct of the activity was much less, though all the managers understood the importance of getting into production quickly, and that ownership of the design is carried through into production. For those firms that use an integrated product development approach, production start-up was not perceived to be a main cause of problems. Consistent with many other NPD activities, the criticality of this activity is affected by the potential volume of products, and their relative level of complexity.

Step 13. Market launch

The importance of the marketing launch of new products varies greatly between the firms, and relates specifically to actual products, and firms' proximity to end-users. For some firms, market launch is a critical activity and little expense is spared in inviting customers and dealers to launch venues. In contrast, for some firms market launch usually meant ensuring that the sales literature was in place and few had a marketing department.

Some questions to ask

Which of the 13 steps do you use?
Be sure that you are not missing out any vital step or are using one that is not needed.

Which of the 13 steps do you find most difficulty to use?
It is usually the 'front end' ones, especially the market and business assessments.
It is these that play a large part in developing products that are successful in the
market.

The stage gate process

The second model of the NPD process that has found increasing favour
with practitioners is the stage gate process shown in Fig. 5.2. The model is
a means of identifying and controlling development risk, which has two
forms:

- **Continuation risk**: the cost of continuing a product development.
- **Abandonment risk**: loss of revenue from products cancelled before
  launch.

These two risks are totally integrated. By breaking the development process
into stages and placing 'go' and 'no-go' gates, or decision criteria points on
each stage, the decision to continue or abandon a development programme
may be better analysed. The stages do not have to follow the 13-step process
as this serves a different purpose. Typically the stage gate process would
have the following characteristics:

- **Several stages**: usually between three and seven stages.
- **Decision gates**: each stage is followed by a decision point or gate.
- **Cross boundaries**: it would cross departmental functions and
  boundaries.
- **Multi-disciplinary**: because the programme and the decisions run
  across functional boundaries, a multi-disciplinary team is essential.
- **Speed and quality**: it must be designed for speedy and high-quality
  execution.

In terms of the strengths and weaknesses of this approach, the process
has yielded the following comments from practitioners.

Strengths

- Improves product development success rates.
- Earlier detection of failures.
- Decisions are more rigorous and transparent.
- Continuous measures of project status.
- Customer oriented and driven.

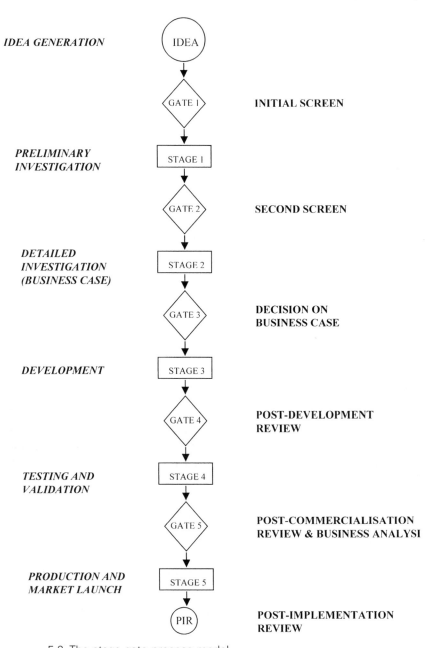

5.2 The stage gate process model.

- Improved teamwork and better communication.
- Reduced recycling and re-work.
- Better market launch.
- Better time management and reduced cycle time.

Weaknesses

- Too much reliance on interfunctional co-operation.
- It takes too long.
- It stifles creativity.
- There is a lack of real control.
- There are problems in defining the 'go' and 'no-go' measures.
- It is limited to certain types of product development.

Some questions to ask

Would a stage gate method be of use to you?
The answer is probably yes as it is now being adopted by both large and small companies.

5.6   Other key influences

One of the key findings of the applied research programme is that the nature of the product under development largely determines the business processes required for successful development. The main areas that companies need to address in order to improve their NPD performance are the integration of the product development activities and the quality of the development process. A greater need for an integrated approach and a high-quality process will be affected by the following:

- **Product complexity**: as the product becomes more structurally (more parts, more technologies, more interfaces, etc) and functionally (more functions both explicit and implicit) complex, then the greater the need for integration for successful development.
- **Product newness**: the newer the product is to the company and to the market, the greater the need for integration for successful development. Newness is related directly to the risk involved in the development. The greater the internal risk to the development (owing to unfamiliarity) and the greater the external risk (owing to customers' lack of knowledge of the product), the greater is the need for the elements of integration for successful product development.

- **Product type**: requirements for the integrating activities will vary according to whether the product is assembly, materials/chemicals or software based.
- **Commercial constraints**: where commercial constraints such as time, development and product costs, legislation, etc, impose on the development, the integration factors become more critical to successful development.
- **Volume**: there is a greater need for integration when products are produced in greater numbers.

Some questions to ask

Where do your current products lie on the structural/functional complexity matrix?
Try to position them in relation to the examples given.

How will any proposed new development affect this positioning?
If you can, try to anticipate the required changes and implement them.

Do you specifically assess a development's newness and risk?
If not then you should. It may be that it should be part of any stage gate process you use.

Do you specifically assess commercial constraints and risk?
Again, if not then you should. Use the 13-step process.

5.7   The use of the ATM

This section describes the ways, or modes, in which the ATM may be used to improve NPD performance. The detail of its operation and application is described in Part III. Here we are concerned with what it can do and how the output might be interpreted. The ATM is a system that relates a company's NPD activities and process to the complexities of a specific product development and the market in which it is to be placed. In this way both the internal and external influences are taken into account:

The ATM has been validated on some 90 separate developments both in the authors' collaborating companies and in a range of NPD good practice companies (including Murata, Nissan, Sony and Sumitomo in Japan) that were unfamiliar with its development. Practitioners found the instrument relatively easy to use. The ATM testing has covered:

- Comparing successful developments from different companies (benchmarking).

- Successful/less successful development comparisons within specific companies.
- Post-development review of a specific development.
- Pre-development assessment.

It is the introduction of the complexity measures that allows a 'like-with-like' comparison to be made between apparently dissimilar products. The ATM runs in Microsoft Access and has an Excel output and may be used by an individual or better still, by a team or group.

Typical outputs

Integrating activities

Figure 9.4 in Chapter 9 shows an output for the integrating activities. As can be seen, they are distributed around the Excel spider chart using the 1–7 scales that are contained within the software system. This diagram shows the output for a non-woven fibre-based product and has a successful and an unsuccessful product superimposed on it.

The immediately obvious item is the lack of use of the tools and techniques and the formal methods that would be found in an engineering-based organisation. This is not a problem as this profile is typical of such a company. Both products' profiles follow the same pattern but the successful one shows a much greater commitment to the development project in terms of process issues, especially in following procedures, general team issues and supplier and customer integration.

Key process stages

The key process stage output for the successful product is shown in Fig. 9.5. This has two profiles on it, one showing the criticality of the process stages and the other showing the proficiency with which they were carried out. The proficiency and criticality have a good match but there is still room for improvement. If you also run the analysis for an unsuccessful product the two outputs may be compared to identify performance gaps.

The authors' collaborating companies have used the ATM to determine the changes needed to improve their NPD environment. Examples of these results are greater adherence to NPD procedures, total co-location, introducing structured systems and information support systems, formal assessment procedures and proposal evaluation, improved programme management, introduction of detailed commercial appraisal into the NPD process and team leadership development. These are described in the case studies in Part IV.

Applications of the ATM

Four applications of the ATM that companies have found useful are described.

Post-development review of a specific development

This is one of the best uses of the ATM. It requires that a specific development programme be reviewed using the ATM to give the review a rigorous structure. In this mode it is not essential that the software programme be used, the ATM format is sufficient to give the review a coherent structure. Use in group mode is especially useful here as the views of a wide variety of people and/or functions can be quite revealing. The results should form the basis of performance improvement programmes.

Successful/less successful development comparisons within a company

This is similar to the example given above, and if used critically and constructively will be rewarding. As with the post-development review, the results should lead to positive action in terms of performance improvement.

Pre-development assessment

Several of the authors' companies have used the ATM in a predictive mode by substituting 'what if' questions for the 'what is' questions. In this type of application, differences, conflicts and incongruities are highlighted at an early stage. These can then be addressed, resolved or accommodated.

Comparing successful developments from different companies (benchmarking)

This was the original purpose in developing the ATM. The aim is to be able to compare products of similar complexities even if they are of a different nature. To use this application you need to complete the software programme and send the results to us. A brief report comparing your results to the research database will be returned to you.

5.8   References and indicative reading

'Benchmarking the firm's critical success factors in new product development', R G Cooper and E J Kleinschmidt, *Journal of Product Innovation Management*, **12**: 374–391, November (1995).

Knowledge Amplification, Jun Numata, Sony's Innovations in Management Series (1996).

'Measuring product development success and failure: a framework defining success and failure', J E Hultink and H S J Robben, *The PDMA Handbook of New Product Development*, Wiley, New York, pp. 455–461 (1996).

'Metrics: a practical example', Leland R Beaumont, *The PDMA Handbook of New Product Development*, Wiley, New York, pp. 463–485 (1996).

New Products Management (5th edn), M Crawford, Richard D Irwin, Chicago (1997).

'PDMA success measurement project: recommended measures of development success and failure', Abbie Griffin and Albert Page, *Journal of Product Innovation Management*, **13**: 478–496 (1996).

Winning at New Products: Accelerating the Process from Idea to Launch, R G Cooper, Cambridge, MA, Second Edition (1993).

Part II

Practical application

6

Application of NPD strategy

This section focuses on the practical aspects of the new product development strategy approaches (as described in section 3). This strategic analysis follows a structured process as shown in the flowchart in Appendix 4. The flowchart is broken into several phases:

- **Phase 1: Initial review.** The definition of the need for a strategic review.
- **Phase 2: External review.** The identification of the key external factors that will affect product development success.
- **Phase 3: Strategy options.** The various options, in terms of the general approaches that companies take in developing new products.
- **Phase 4: Strategy focus.** Where are the effort and resources going to be focused? The actual strategy that is put into action.

These notes should be read in conjunction with the flowchart in Appendix 4. However, we do recommend that the 'theory' in section 3 be read first.

6.1 Phase 1: The initial review

This sets the scene in terms of how much (or little) needs to be done in addressing your strategic needs.

Do you have an NPD strategy?

No: Then the immediate question is why not? Perhaps you feel that you do not need one or that the issue appears to be too complicated or involved. As with any other area of strategy, there is evidence that strategic planning will aid success and also evidence that without it you are much more likely to fail. Questions to ask here are:

Some questions to ask

What benefits will you gain if you develop a NPD strategy?
Will the company be more secure, profitable, etc.?

What dangers do you face if you do not develop a NPD strategy?
Will you miss opportunities or, worse still, threats?

In the flowchart go to the step asking whether you wish to develop a NPD strategy.
Yes: The only question here is whether you are satisfied with your NPD strategy. Go to the next step.

Do you wish to develop a NPD strategy?

No: Then stop the process here (or read on to see whether you do need to develop a strategy!).
Yes: Then conduct a complete review of NPD strategy. Go to that step in the flowchart.

Are you satisfied with the NPD strategy?

No: Then you will be best served by conducting a complete review of your NPD strategy so continue through the flowchart (we recommend that you do this in conjunction with a review of the integrating activities and development process).
Yes: Then stop the process here (or read on to see whether you should review strategy).

6.2   Phase 2: The external review

Do you have an up-to-date analysis of your competitive position?

Developing new products is a long-term activity and needs to be done within the framework of the future competitive environment (as much as anyone can foresee it). The tools at your disposal for conducting an external appraisal are many and varied and it is impossible for most businesses to use them all. You need to define which are most appropriate (not the easiest) to use and use a mixture of hard analysis and intuition ('gut feeling'). Do not simply rely on what the customer tells you as that addresses only today's problems.

Wherever possible, the external appraisal should be linked closely with any market research and business analysis activities; it should certainly be part of the annual strategic planning process.

If you have already conducted this analysis then check whether any of the appraisal tools and techniques outlined here that you do not use might be of use to you.

6.3 Phase 3: The strategy options

These options fall into two broad approaches which are not mutually exclusive:

- **Reactive NPD strategies**: deal with pressures as they occur, such as copying a successful product of a competitor.
- **Proactive NPD strategies**: identify and capture opportunities and try to be first in the market-place.

A comparison of the two approaches is given in Table 3.2 on p. 35.

What is needed for a reactive strategy?

Reactive strategies focus on making changes in existing products to counteract a competitor's successful launch, quick copying on a 'me too' basis, producing an improved copy and purposefully reacting to customers' requests. At its heart are responsiveness, agility, flexibility and efficiency. Being close to the customer is essential for this strategy to work well.

What are the advantages/disadvantages of a reactive strategy?

The main danger here is that being too close to the customer can lead to too great a dependency on a specific customer and result in a lack of product change. It also tends to lead to low added-value products. On the up side, risks are generally lower and business futures are more predictable.

What is needed for a proactive strategy?

This can revolve around investment for the longer term future (R&D, marketing) such as finding a consumer need and then producing a product to meet it. Alternatively, the entrepreneurial route is chosen (an individual makes an idea happen or the company purchases a company with new technology, products or markets).

What are the advantages/disadvantages of a proactive strategy?

With a proactive NPD strategy, a company must control risk and at the same time encourage creative development. The basic problem is that the organisation tends to nullify creative endeavour. Managers must develop an organisation that is disciplined and yet creative. This can be done but requires fully trained and business-aware people at all levels, with clear objectives and top level support.

6.4   Phase 4: Strategy focus

On which of our current products should we focus?

Use the BCG (section 3) and/or the Ansoff matrix analysis (section 3) to help you define where your scarce resources might best be deployed.

On which aspect(s) of our future potential should we focus?

Use the Ansoff matrix analysis to determine this.

Are we dealing with a specific product?

Yes: Then we can focus on it and devote appropriate resources to its development.
No: If this is the case, then a more comprehensive programme of work is needed, especially when reviewing the integrating activities and the development process.

Do we develop the product ourselves?

Yes: This is the internal development option relying on the skills, capabilities and competencies within the company. If these do not already exist, then they must be developed or brought in. Changing these 'core' skills can be a difficult and a long-term process.
No: Then consider the other options.

Do we 'buy' our way into the business?

Yes: The routes here are essentially all external, including acquisition, joint ventures, partnerships and, less common in product development terms, turn around.
No: Then you have run out of options!

7

Measuring development performance

7.1 Introduction

Measuring the performance of your product development process and activities brings with it the basic problems associated with any form of measuring. This starts with defining what it is that we wish to know and why we wish to know this measure. This is followed by the reality of what we can measure and whether what we want to know coincides with what we can actually measure. If not, how can we get at what we really need? By understanding performance metrics and being able to apply them, you are more likely to bring about continuous improvement in NPD success rates. This section tries to answer the question:

'What do we mean by NPD performance measurement and how do we apply it?'

We now categorise performance metrics in two ways: **internal** and **external**. The internal performance metric comprises the **process outcomes**. These include meeting specification, being on time, being on budget, etc. They cover both technical and non-technical metrics.

The external performance metric comprises:

- **Customer outcomes**: these are primarily customer acceptance and satisfaction.
- **Business outcomes**: including profit, sales turnover, market share.

It is these metrics that concern us.

Before starting on a review of your performance measures and system/process, it is worth trying to answer clearly the following questions:

Some questions to ask

What benefits will measuring your NPD performance bring?
It is important that you know why you are attempting to measure performance before you decide what to measure.

Will the measures help you to improve the overall process?
Performance metrics must serve the dual purpose of telling you how well your process is performing and how things may be improved.

Do you use internal and external metrics?
It is important that both are used in the context of NPD and that the latter is not viewed as a general business measure.

Can you relate internal and external success?
This is extremely difficult to do well. There is clear evidence that failure internally will probably lead to failure externally whereas good internal management is more likely to lead to external success.

Which metrics are most important to NPD?
From the general metrics that you have defined, extract those that relate both directly and indirectly to your NPD strategy, activities and process.

Do you really need to measure these?
This is the most fundamental question of all. If it is not that important to you then why waste time, energy and resources developing a system and its metrics?

If you do measure, what are you going to do with the results?
Having decided that certain metrics are important, double check them by defining what action they will prompt once a measure has been produced.

'Who needs to know what, why and what will they do with it?'

Again, if you cannot see a strong and consistent use for it, then why do it?

What is your development lead-time?
Clearly, long development lead-times (e.g. ten years and more) demand different approaches from short lead-times. Short lead-times lend themselves to rapid feedback from the market. Long lead-times demand rigorous internal efficiency and effectiveness and constant checking on the market to ensure the product still 'fits' it.

7.2   Reviewing your performance measurement process

These notes should be read in conjunction with the flowchart in Appendix 5.

Do you have an efficient and effective NPD performance measurement system?

Yes: This should be a system dedicated to the NPD activities and process and not a simple extension of other business measurement systems. If you do have one then review it against the conceptual process models.

No: Then use the conceptual process models to develop one. It does not have to be over-formal and can be refined over a period of time. So:

'Let's measure what we need to know and not what we can'

What are the key drivers for your business?

What are the key business drivers that are going to make the most significant contribution to your competitive advantage? This is vitally important as there can be conflicts, e.g. customer satisfaction versus cost.

Do you relate these key business drivers to business metrics?

Yes: Then carry on with the flowchart.
No: Relate your key business performance metrics to your business drivers (and vice versa).

Do you have NPD metrics that relate to the business metrics?

Yes: This is to confirm the metrics. Ask yourself why and what action will be taken as a result of obtaining this information. This should ensure that you only retain the relevant (not the easiest, please!) metrics for use. Review them periodically to ensure that they are still relevant and to satisfy yourself that what you have is what you need for the future.
No: You must develop metrics and the means of applying them. Otherwise you will have no basis for assessing the impact of improvement methods and programmes (Section 8 on improving NPD performance will help here).

Integrate the metrics and the measurement system

The measurement system you have (or have developed) must deliver the required metrics. To do this, the two must be integrated as a seamless whole. The easiest way of doing this is to use the key metrics as the focus of refining the measurement system you have developed (this is the review process referred to in the flowchart).

Are you measuring what is essential?

This is a check step in the overall process.
Yes: Then carry on applying the metrics but make sure that you review them periodically.

No: You must develop the metrics that you have.

Apply the measurement system and metrics

It is not unusual to find that having done all the above work, companies do not actually apply and/or maintain their system. The main reasons for this are:

- Boredom with the discipline that is needed for continuous application.
- Lack of immediate feedback and/or impact – it may take at least one and possibly more development cycles before the true value of the work becomes apparent.

Are the metrics and measurement system giving practical results?

There must be clear evidence that the work is useful in improving the long-term success rate of developments.

Yes: Then carry on applying them but make sure that you review them periodically. Set a date for a review.

No: You must review the whole process.

8

Improving development performance

This Section is concerned with the practical review and improvement of your product development performance. It follows a structured process as shown in the flowchart in Appendix 6. The flowchart is broken into several phases:

- *Phase 1: Pre-review assessment.* This covers the measurement and analysis of your current performance level.
- *Phase 2: Review focus.* The definition of the focus of the review and improvement work.
- *Phase 3: Review method.* The alternative methods of carrying out the review and assessment.
- *Phase 4: Review scope.* Defining the actual scope of the improvement programme.
- *Phase 5: Programme planning.* Planning the change programme to address the issues identified in Phase 4.
- *Phase 6: Programme execution.* Implementing the change programme developed in Phase 5.
- *Phase 7: Programme evaluation.* Evaluating the impact of the change programme carried out in Phase 6.

8.1 Phase 1: Pre-review assessment

Do you wish to improve your NPD performance level?

Yes: Then carry out an initial assessment of what it is that you are trying to do and why you wish to do it. At this stage it need not be detailed but more setting the scene or the general area/scope of the review. This is setting the strategic framework for the action/review to be defined later by this process.

Some questions to ask

Why do you wish to improve performance?
Be sure that you have a clear, and a generally agreed, perception of why you are starting this process.

What are our aims in doing this?
Clarify your aims. Be clear about what it is that you are trying to achieve.

How pressing is the need?
Is it short or long term or both?

Is it likely to be specific or comprehensive?
Try to make an initial evaluation of the breadth and depth of the review.

What outcomes do we desire?
By defining the desired and expected outcomes you will have a much greater chance of ensuring that the overall programme succeeds.

How will we know that we have succeeded?
Keep in mind that you will need to set measurable targets.

Can you measure your current NPD performance level?

No: Then we strongly advise you to develop, introduce and apply a performance measurement system and related metrics. As a guide to doing this we would refer you to Section 7. The three main questions to be asked here are:

Some questions to ask

What would be the focus of the system?
There is a clear difference between measuring internal efficiency (time, budget, specification met, etc) and external effectiveness (market share, customer acceptance, profitability, etc).

What resources will you commit to a performance measurement system?
For any system that you introduce there will be a 'cost' in terms of finance, time, energy, etc. As with all such systems, the aim here is for maximum reward for minimum effort. Ensuring that the broad strategic aims have been defined (above) will help you to achieve this.

What do we measure?
Avoid falling into the trap of identifying and using what may be easily measured. Keep the overall strategy in mind, define what it is that you need to know and then find a way to measure it. Some of the key performance metrics do not lend themselves to easy measurement but if an attribute has to be measured then a way of measuring it must be found.

Yes: The only point here is whether your performance measurement system is adequate. If the outline strategy defined above points to the need for a comprehensive review then it is probably worth reviewing the measurement system and its metrics as well.

Assess the current level of NPD performance

This step in the process really acts as a check or guideline to ensure that improvement is needed and, if so, in broad terms what it is that needs to be done. At this stage you are not trying to set improvement targets, you merely wish to confirm whether the general level of performance is acceptable. Questions to ask here include:

Some questions to ask

How good is your internal efficiency?
Do you manage developments well in terms of budgets, time targets, etc.?

How good is your external effectiveness?
Do your products do well in the market-place and make profits?

Are you looking at product-specific or general levels of performance?
These require different approaches.

Are you satisfied with the current performance level?

No: Then proceed through the review process.
Yes: Then stop the process at this point but set a date for the next review of the NPD performance. Do something more constructive!

8.2 Phase 2: Review focus

Do you know where improvements may be made?

Some questions to ask

Conduct a complete review of your NPD activities and process?
This will cover everything involved in your development process. In the authors' experience this is only needed periodically, usually if your performance level is poor.

Focus on the integrating activities only?
This simply looks at the activities and functions found within the development environment.

Focus on the NPD process only?
This addresses process issues only.

Focus on one specific aspect of the NPD performance only?
If you choose this option then you already have a reasonably good idea of where the improvement emphasis needs to be placed.

(The first three options involve the use of the ATM.)

Yes: Then proceed to the step of the flowchart concerned with defining the scope of the improvement programme.

No: Then the key issue is to determine the focus. This will be achieved by following the flowchart and using the ATM.

Do you wish to carry out an overall review?

Yes: The aim here is to start the process of defining what it is that needs to be reviewed and improved.

No: Continue through the flowchart.

Review the integrating activities only?

Yes: Use the ATM.

No: Go to the next stage of the flowchart.

Review the development process only?

Yes: Use the ATM.

No: Go to the next stage of the flowchart.

Focus on a specific aspect?

Yes: Then proceed to the step of the flowchart concerned with defining the improvement area(s) and scope.

No: If you are at this step and you are still not sure what needs to be done then you should ask yourself the following questions:

Some questions to ask

Should you re-start the whole process?
Are you at this stage because you are not sure of what you are trying to do or are things OK as they are?

Should you use the ATM to carry out a full review?
Are you just undecided about what you should do? If the answer is yes then a full review is probably worthwhile.

Should you stop the process altogether?
Are you sure that effort put into trying to improve the process would not be warranted?

8.3   Phase 3: Review method

The alternative ways of using the ATM are described in Sections 9 and 10.

8.4   Phase 4: Review scope

Define the improvement area(s) and scope

This is another 'check' step. Do not attempt to set improvement targets at this point. What is needed here is confirmation that the output from the above is really what is required. Check this against the overall strategy defined in the first step. Also conduct a provisional check that you have not over-reached yourselves in terms of the scope of a potential improvement programme and your ability to support it.

Set improvement targets and re-confirm the aims

Try to set clear, unambiguous and achievable improvement targets. Make sure that these reflect the defined aims.

8.5   Phase 5: Programme planning

Communicate the change aims and gain acceptance

This step has two primary purposes. Any change will have an impact on personnel, so early knowledge will help in the acceptance of the change programme to be developed later. Any other issues/problems that need to be addressed within the change programme should be identified.

Some questions to ask

Who will approve the changes and the commitment of resources?
Without the positive support of these people, the programme will struggle to achieve its aims.

Who will be affected by the possible changes?
Get them all involved, or at least get their acceptance that things need to change.

Who will effect the change?
Bring in the programme team as early as possible.

Establish the change programme team

Some questions to ask

Can the programme be carried out by an individual?
If the answer is yes, then do not set up a team.

Is a programme team needed?
If the answer is yes, then choose the team carefully using technical, functional and group effectiveness and maintenance criteria.

Develop the change programme

Each company's needs will be specific.

Some questions to ask

Will the programme meet the original aims?
Check this against the aims defined in Phases 1 and 4.

Do the potential gains justify the investment?
Try to put figures on the programme in terms of finance, time, resources, etc. Can you afford to do it?

Is it essential?
Can you afford not to do it?

Communicate the action plans and gain acceptance

- To senior management and resource controllers. Their positive support will be essential.
- To the people who will be affected by the possible changes. Get them all 'on board' as their acceptance will be critical. Time spent here is time well spent.
- To the change team.

8.6   Phase 6: Programme execution

Will the change programme be evaluated?

Yes: Then go to the next step of the process.
No: Then implement the programme but do not be surprised if you cannot measure the effect.

Confirm programme performance measures and targets

Briefly run through the whole of the programme's purpose and targets as a final check before launching the programme.

Execute the programme and monitor results

Programme execution needs to be closely linked with programme monitoring. It is the monitoring process that will reveal many of the key lessons that can be transferred to the next improvement programme.

8.7   Phase 7: Programme evaluation

Review the programme against the targets

This is the step that most companies either fail to do or do poorly. Unless you undertake a review, the full benefit of the programme and the learning from it will not be realised.

Extract key lessons for future use

Extract the key lessons (especially the transferable ones) from the above step.

Some questions to ask

What did we do well?
Identify the key lessons and build them into future programmes.
What did we do badly?
Identify them and remove them from future programmes.
Is there anything that we can use regularly?
Transfer lessons to other programme areas or into the general strategy.

Re-start the process

Set the date for the next review (and keep to it!).

Part III

The assessment tool and methodology

9

Using the assessment tool
and methodology

9.1 Introduction

The assessment tool and methodology (ATM) is a structured method designed to assist the improvement of a company's NPD performance. It provides a framework whereby a company can evaluate its past product development performance and select or confirm potential areas on which to focus their improvement effort. Its actual use is described in Section 10.

Two significant areas are recognised for improving NPD performance; integrating activities (e.g. team working, formal development procedures, computer-based tools and formal methods), which allow effective communication of information in the development process, and the product development process (from initial screening to market launch), which should be carried out where relevant and to the desired proficiency. The ATM evaluates the performance of both areas indicating, through a series of graphs, where performance may be improved.

9.2 Using the ATM

The ATM is designed to be used in any of four specific modes:

- Formal appraisal of a past product development.
- Internal benchmarking via a successful product versus a less successful product.
- External benchmarking of a development against external best practice.
- Pre-development assessment.

In each case the objective of the appraisal is to spot the comparatively low performance scores for both the integrating activities and the product development stage performance and to focus on their improvement.

Post-development review

Most firms have a history of both successes and 'failures' in product development. Learning from mistakes and building on achievements is essential for companies wishing to improve their NPD performance. In the past, well-established firms such as Ford UK, with its documented failure of a power train in the late 1980s, had to review their product development activities radically in order to produce world class products. The approach it took was a post-development review where the product development was critically analysed to establish lessons learned allowing hindsight to play a role in understanding how future development might be improved.

The ATM provides a structured framework for post-development review and allows firms to increase their product development success rate by increasing the chances of success with each subsequent programme. The questionnaire can be completed either by development managers or by teams where the mean scores are used. The latter method is beneficial in resolving areas of conflict within product development teams.

Internal benchmark: successful/less successful comparison

Comparing product successes with less successful products within a company provides useful insights into potential reasons for success and failure. The ATM has been used extensively in this mode with the authors' collaborating companies and has proved useful in formalising lessons learned. It encourages companies to focus on areas that they know have benefited them in the past.

In order that benchmark comparisons may be valid, products of similar complexity and newness should be chosen. The ATM evaluates both the complexity and the newness of the products to assist in the process. Performance scores are obtained for both the successful and less successful products. Where there is a significant 'gap' in performance, the company may wish to focus its improvement actions on this area.

External benchmark of NPD best practice

Companies wishing to stay ahead of the competition can improve their performance by looking outside their organisations and learning from other market sectors where they can make use of the best practices of other companies. The ATM enables successful products of similar complexity and newness to be compared. Performance of the development of these 'analogous' products can then be used to establish performance gaps and areas where improvement may be beneficial.

Pre-development review

The ATM may be used prior to the initiation of a development programme to allow key issues to be defined and addressed.

9.3 Structure of the questionnaire

The questionnaire is presented in two formats, paper and Microsoft Access based, and is divided into four parts:

- **Part 1: Product selection and company information**. This asks you to select a product for evaluation and gives a series of measures to evaluate your performance.
- **Part 2: Complexity, newness and commercial constraints assessment**. This section evaluates the newness and complexity of your product. These measures are used in the benchmarking exercises in order to select similar products.
- **Part 3: Integration activity evaluation**. This section evaluates the company's perceived performance in 19 activities which assist the integration of the product development.
- **Part 4: Process stage evaluation**. The final part of the ATM asks participants to assess the criticality of a number of development stages from initial screening through to market launch and then to evaluate the proficiency to which each of the stages were carried out.

9.4 Using Microsoft Access

The most fruitful way of using the assessment tool is through the Microsoft Access software package. Questions are asked in Access where the data can be stored. On completion of the questionnaire, the results are transferred to an Excel spreadsheet where you are able to produce and print a number of relevant graphs.

9.5 Interpreting the graphs

Five graphs are created showing your NPD performance and product characteristics:

- Internal and external product development performance.
- Product newness.
- Product complexity.
- Integrating activities performance.
- Process stages performance.

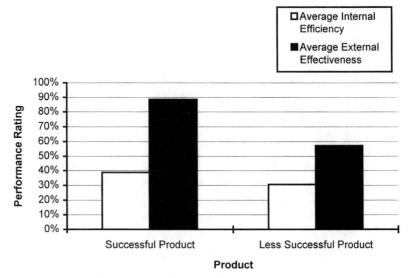

9.1 Internal/external product development performance.

Internal and external product development performance

The graph in Fig. 9.1 provides a quick means of assessing how well your company has met certain product development performance criteria. (A score of 100% means your selected performance criteria were fully met.) There are two distinct sets of measures:

- **Internal efficiency** relates to measures of how well the product development was carried out within the organisation prior to launch, e.g. quality, cost, time and performance *v.* specification.
- **External effectiveness** relates to measures of performance of the product in the market-place, e.g. market position, sales, ROI/IRR, customer satisfaction, break-even time.

Products that are successful will tend to have higher scores of both internal and external development performance compared to their less successful counterparts. High scores of internal efficiency do not always equate to high scores of external effectiveness.

Product newness

Figure 9.2 shows the percentage newness of products from both the company and market/customer perspective. (A score of 100% means that

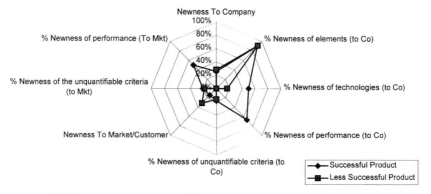

9.2 Product newness profile.

the product is a totally radical step away from anything previously developed by the company or purchased by the market.) This profile assists with the benchmarking process. In order to make valid comparisons, products should be of similar newness. The example graph also shows that the successful product was considerably newer to the company than the less successfull product. These products may not make suitable benchmarking partners. The newness metrics are described below.

Newness of the product to the company

Five measures are given for the newness of the product to the company. They distinguish between the 'amount' of the product which is considered totally new and that used on previous products (which simplify the product development):

- **% newness to the company:** a quick measure of perceived product newness to the company.
- **% newness of product elements:** identifies the percentage of the new product elements relative to the total number of elements in the product.
- **% newness of technologies:** identifies the percentage of new technological disciplines relative to the total number of technologies used in the product.
- **% newness of performance:** identifies the percentage of performance criteria new to the company relative to the total number of performance criteria for that product.
- **% newness of unquantifiables:** indicates the degree to which the performance criteria (e.g. style, feel) are new to the company. Scores

are weighted according to the importance of each of the unquantifiable criteria.

High levels of product newness to the company indicate that the company is stepping outside its usual area of expertise. Such products require the acquisition of knowledge and tend to be more risky than those products which utilise the company's existing skills and knowledge.

Newness of the product to the customer

Three measures are given for the newness of the product to the market:

- **% newness to the customer:** a measure of the perceived product newness to the customer. High levels of newness to the customer again increase risk of product development.
- **% newness of performance:** identifies the percentage of quantifiable performance criteria that are new to the customer relative to the total number of performance criteria for that product.
- **% newness of 'unquantifiables':** indicates the degree to which the 'unquantifiable' performance criteria (e.g. appearance, style, feel) are considered new to the customer. Scores are weighted according to the importance of each of the unquantifiable criteria.

Product complexity

The profile in Fig. 9.3 is used to assist the benchmarking process (which is only valid where products of similar complexity are compared). In the example in Fig. 9.3, the complexity criteria are well matched. The successful product, however, has greater complexity in the number of performance criteria. (Maximum scores for any of the measures is 10.) Product complexity is measured in three areas:

- Structural.
- Functional.
- Supporting indicators.

Structural complexity

This relates to the composition of the product, its elements and how they relate to each other. There are six measures that describe the product complexity.

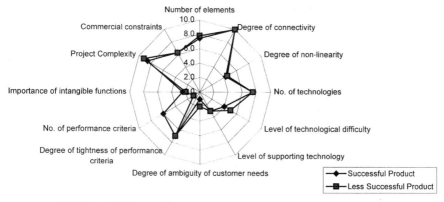

9.3 Complexity profile.

- **Number of elements**: relates to the number of components, assemblies, subsystems of which the product consists.
- **Degree of connectivity**: the number of interfaces between components.
- **Degree of non-linearity**: a measure of the degree to which the relationship between the product's elements is known.
- **Number of technologies**: the number of technologies used to develop the product.
- **Level of technological difficulty**: a measure of the level of sophistication of the technology used to develop the product (e.g. manufacturing equipment, testing equipment).
- **Level of supporting technology**: a measure of the degree to which the development of supporting technologies such as manufacture and test equipment have characterised the development.

Functional complexity

This relates the product to its market and reflects its interaction with the customer.

- **Degree of ambiguity of customer needs**: the degree to which the respondents believe the initial customer specification of the project was ill defined. High scores mean that there is significant ambiguity.
- **Degree of tightness of performance criteria**: the tolerance placed on the performance criteria. Those that are perceived to be tight and demanding receive higher scores.

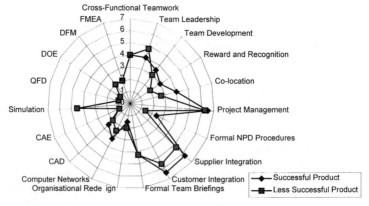

9.4 Integrating activity performance profile.

- **Number of performance criteria**: the number of performance criteria specified for the product.
- **Importance of intangible functions**: the perceived importance of unmeasurable functions of the product such as appearance, style and taste.

Supporting indicators

These are:

- **Project complexity**: relates to the measures such as development time, number of people employed on the project internally and externally to the company.
- **Commercial constraints**: measures the degree to which respondents believe the commercial pressures such as time, product cost, development cost and quality have imposed on the development process.

Integrating activities performance

Figure 9.4 depicts the scores for the integrating activities for a successful/less successful product comparison. The maximum score for any of the activities is 7.

Process stages performance

Figure 9.5 depicts ten major stages in the product development process and the respective perceived criticality and performance of each stage employed. The example graph shows a performance gap between the

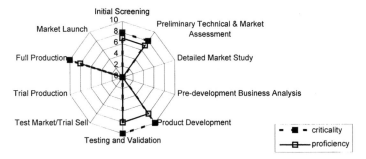

9.5 Process stages performance: criticality versus proficiency (successful product).

criticality and proficiency at each stage, implying that there is scope for improvement even for a successful product.

9.6 The way forward

On completion of the four parts you will be able to produce graphs of your NPD development performance. These can be compared with other products in your organisation. Alternatively, return your results to us and we will compare it with our general database.

10

The CD-ROM software: ATM and NPD flowcharts

10.1 System requirements for running the CD-ROM

486 (minimum)
8Mb RAM (minimum) recommended 32Mb
50Mb available memory and 2Mb graphic adaptor
Monitor: 640 × 480, 256 colour (recommended 800 × 600) – modify via Control Panel
Windows 95 or above (Windows 98 recommended)
Microsoft Excel '97

10.2 About the CD-ROM software

The software package has three principal components:

1. **The ATM questionnaire:** This contains a series of questions relating to product development. The results are stored on a Microsoft Access database.
2. **The ATM graphical analysis:** The results of the questionnaire can be automatically transferred to a Microsoft Excel spreadsheet specifically designed to analyse NPD performance and to produce graphical output for simplified analysis. You will need Excel '97 or above to be able to use the package properly. The spreadsheet examines one product or compares two products.
3. **The NPD flow charts:** There are a number of animated flow charts (as in Appendices 4, 5, and 6) relating to the use of the workbook and the ATM. These can be read directly from the CD-ROM or hard drive and show the flow of activities and decisions when developing an NPD strategy, measurement system or using the ATM.

10.3 Installing the NPD assessment tool

Loading the software from Windows 95/98/NT

1. Insert CD-ROM
2. Go to **My Computer**, select **CD-ROM** drive and double click on **setup**
3. Follow the instructions of the installation wizard.

Do NOT alter directory **C:\ npdtool**

NB For 95/NT only: The program is not put in the registry. Ignore the message that the software has not completed successfully. 95/NT loads more slowly than 98.

10.4   Starting the ATM software

Go to **My Computer**, double click on **C:/** and double click on the **NPDTOOL** folder.
Double click on **npdtool** in NPDTOOL folder.

Using the software

Step 1: Answer the questionnaire

1. At the 'Welcome' page select a product or enter the name of the product you wish to assess.
2. Click **Introduction** if you wish to obtain further details about the tool.
3. Click **Continue**
4. Click **Assess product** and complete the four sections of the questionnaire or click appropriate button to enter the questionnaire at parts 2, 3 or 4.

Step 2: Save the data and open the Excel Spreadsheet

1. At the 'Congratulations' page of the questionnaire choose output selection **Spreadsheet output for Excel**. This saves the data for use in Excel.
2. Choose **Start Excel Now** which automatically runs the spreadsheet **C:/npdtool/newgraph.xls**
3. Now you are in Excel, save the spreadsheet under a new name of your choice. This will ensure you will always have a clean copy of the spreadsheet template.

Step 3: Transfer the data to the Excel Spreadsheet

1. Make sure you are on sheet **Template 1** of Excel newgraph.xls
2. Select **Tools** and choose **first product data** to transfer the text files containing the results of the questionnaire into the Excel spreadsheet.

If you wish to compare a second product then:

3. Return to NPD Tool
4. Choose another product or enter a new set of data for the questionnaire
5. Return to the spreadsheet
6. Make sure you are on sheet **Template 1**
7. Select **Tools** and choose **second product data** to pull your results from Access to Excel.

Step 4: Print the graphs
Printouts can be obtained for both assessment of single products and comparison of two products. These can be obtained by selecting and printing the appropriate pages of the spreadsheet.

To print graph for one product:

1. Select spread sheet labelled **Print Graph Page 1, (1 product)** and print
2. Select spread sheet labelled **Print Graph Page 2, (1 product)** and print

To print graphs for two products:
1. Select spread sheet labelled **Print Graph Page 1, (2 product)** and print
2. Select spread sheet labelled **Print Graph Page 2, (2 product)** and print

10.5   Using the flowchart software

To start the flow charts:
Read the flow charts directly from the CD-ROM or hard drive by double clicking on the icon **NPDflow** in the **NPDTOOL** folder.

Moving around the flow charts:
Click on the 'spots' to move your way through the flow charts. These are animated versions of the flowcharts in Appendices 4, 5 and 6. The relevant section of the workbook is indicated for each item selected.

Part IV

Case studies

Case studies

11.1 J C Bamford Excavators Ltd (Rocester, UK)

- *Use of detailed market and design briefs.*
- *Adherence to procedures.*
- *Dedicated design teams.*
- *The use of post-development (or post-mortem) reviews.*
- *Continuous improvement philosophy.*

Company background

J C Bamford (JCB) started in a lock-up garage in Uttoxeter in 1945 when Joseph Cyril Bamford set about creating the very first JCB product, a tipping trailer. Over 50 years later, JCB now has seven factories and 3,400 employees building over 22,000 machines per year in nine different product ranges. With exports accounting for 70% of sales, JCB is a clear technological and market leader in many of the 140 countries world-wide to which it sells.

This case study focuses on the development of two products from JCB's Telescopic Handler range, one of which was immensely successful (Project B), becoming the world's best-selling telescopic handler, while the other (Project A) had far less impact on machine sales. Both projects were major updates to existing products with all personnel involved being totally co-located in both cases. For both developments new product procedures were in place. In the case of the less successful product, these were not closely followed. Post-development review led to this being identified as a major reason for the problems. This led to the procedures and improvements being strictly adhered to for the Project B development which has been an outstanding success.

Key issues

The main issue for JCB was the finding of a way and/or method whereby it could introduce a continuous, overall improvement philosophy that was specific to the company's products. It found that the use of post-development review was the most appropriate method for this.

Key findings

The use of an open and collaborative post-development review process has yielded tremendous benefits to JCB's development programmes. By addressing a significant number of aspects of Project A's problems, clear lessons were drawn. However, that was only part of the process. The main impact was achieved by finding ways to address these issues in a comprehensive and integrated way. While the identified issues were wide ranging, fairly simple approaches and solutions were adopted that ensured that the same problems were eliminated from, or significantly reduced for, future development programmes.

Post-development review is now an established part of JCB's overall product development procedure and system. This is shown by Steve Yianni's final comment on Project B's review:

'Whilst the project has been a success, by working together, I am sure we can show an improvement in the areas listed here for our future product introductions'.

Project A: The less successful product

The development of this product was completed in 1995 and a post-mortem review was conducted on 20 March 1996 to determine process improvements for future development programmes. The meeting was attended by cross-functional representatives, all of whom had been involved in the project. All the comments at the meeting were listed together with the action needed to be taken to improve the process for the future. In all, 27 key items were listed. The issues ranged from basic engineering problems to ones of team-work and lack of control, focus and commitment.

With such a wide-ranging variety of issues, the formal NPD procedure was reviewed and found to be satisfactory but needed to be followed more closely together with improvements in the way the project was managed and the way in which the people worked together. Further discussions also led to the identification of three other key points of action:

- Programme content should be largely self-contained through detailed briefs from marketing and design.
- Programmes should be allocated to a dedicated and focused design team.
- Multi-disciplinary involvement is essential throughout a programme.

Specific actions were taken to ensure that all these identified issues were addressed.

Project B: The successful product

It was agreed that the project had been a success, with product introduction obtained four months after project initiation. This was mainly put down to the following:

- Project content largely contained (through marketing and design briefs).
- A dedicated, focused design team.
- Multi-disciplinary involvement throughout.

The review of Project B was aimed at analysing the good and not so good elements of the project, especially in terms of the lessons learnt, and applied, from Project A. In comparing the issues that had been analysed previously on Project A, the review meeting agreed that significant progress had been demonstrated on 18 of the 27 issues raised. Project B had, therefore, addressed two-thirds of those issues raised on Project A. However, it was recognised that Project B revealed that further areas of improvement could be made.

11.2   BBA Friction Ltd (Cleckheaton, UK)

- *Clearly defined new product strategy.*
- *Use of sophisticated, computer-based product development information system.*
- *Team building, team-work and the use of team briefings.*
- *Moving outside the project/programme framework.*

Company background

BBA Friction Ltd develops and manufactures brake lining materials and the full liner shoe assemblies. The site at Cleckheaton employs some 450 people and covers the light vehicle brake activity. BBA Ltd is a world leader in brake lining technology and recognised throughout the industry as a world class company.

BBA Friction develops products for both the original equipment and the replacement markets and has a wide product base. It is closely tied in to all the major vehicle manufacturers and this causes them extreme difficulties in product development strategies. It is faced with meeting quite disparate vehicle brake specification requirements with vehicle companies and countries defining not only the actual performance specifications, but many of the raw materials that are allowed or excluded from particular formulations. In the past most of its development activity has been within the project framework. This has caused a problem in meeting time scales and deadlines as every development is effectively a totally new one.

Key issues

The key issues for BBA Friction were:

- Trying to move out of development within the project framework to one that was more generic and flexible.
- Moving away from the 'black art' typically associated with this type of industry. While there is a high level of technical and engineering capability, much of the development work is done intuitively relying on experiential interpretation as opposed to structured experimentation. While this intuitive approach is useful, a much more rigorous, robust and structured approach to the development processes was needed.
- Because of the diversity of specifications and because of the high number of potential combination of ingredients (a formulation typically will include 12–15 different ingredients), keeping track of the information and the influence of changes on performance criteria was exceedingly difficult.
- One of the problems was the division between chemists, engineers, sales and marketing and the manufacturing operation. This was partly historical in that they had all basically worked separately and partly geographical in that the R&D operation was located some 300 metres away from the manufacturing and administrative base.

The work of the authors' staff fell into three areas:

- Supporting the development of the product development strategy and approach.
- Working with the company on team building and particularly the issue of the confidence of technical staff in the changing market circumstances.
- The key issue of the information and information processing.

Product development strategy and approach

The reliance on development within the project framework, as stated above, resulted in long lead-times and high resource activity for every development. After reviewing its overall strategy, the company decided to move outside the project framework, i.e. to identify key dimensions of the products and the product development activities and to work towards these. This would then push the development work beyond the limits that would be expected from any single project development and thus, when a new business arose, the company would have the broad parameters already defined and know how to get to them.

Extensive team meetings held with chemists, engineers and sales people identified the key issues and the specification criteria from the whole range of BBA's customers. This led to defining a series of criteria, not only in terms of the actual performance, but the likely extreme measure attainable, yet beyond the current expectations of the customer. These criteria were then categorised within the influencing factors over which BBA had control, e.g. the chemistry, the material processing, the manufacturing systems. From such deliberation a programme framework emerged using methodologies such as Taguchi. Defining a broad series of development programmes allowed the work to continue within the action directly needed by the commercial activities. This approach has begun to pay dividends as some projects have arisen where the specification is within the framework that has already been developed and only minor adjustments have been needed in terms of formulation and manufacturing capability.

Team building and individual development

BBA felt that a team-oriented approach would be needed to meet the new challenges. Issues of segregation had caused problems in the past, as had the problem of the move away from the project framework into strategic development. These required placing a greater emphasis on systems and information. Some, who saw this as a threat, preferred to work in the more intuitive way of the past.

A specially organised team-building session of the individual R&D development chemists and engineers identified the main issues that were involved. A wide range of issues and topics was highlighted. These were then compiled and circulated to all who had taken part and each person was asked to put them in order of priority. The results were collated and found to be largely unanimous. This proved to be very successful in that many of the concerns that were of the lower ranking were basically dismissed as being inconsequential and just two or three high ranking items were identified for further work. These were:

• Greater integration between chemists, engineers and sales people.
• A review of R&D resources allied to the new development strategy.

- The implementation of a computer-based information system relating to the new development environment.

Setting up regular meetings of interdisciplinary teams has been a most successful part of the BBA activity. The second item was addressed during the annual budgeting round. Resources were allocated by the senior management to the third item.

The material development initiative (MDI) system

With the help of the computing department, management drew up a specification for the complete information flow from first customer contact to detailed specification and development activity. The design of the MDI proposal allowed development people to track individual developments, rather like a staged process, and enabled them to conduct detailed statistical analysis of the relationships among the key variables in the development of friction materials.

The design of the MDI took some 12 months and involved chemists, engineers, sales, manufacturing systems and production personnel. The resources allocated to the computing aspects of this came from the central computing services. The MDI was promoted not only by the R&D team but also by the senior management within BBA and this high profile meant that things happened fairly quickly. The current state is that the trial computer-based system run in tandem with the paper-based system has worked well.

The computer-based system has been further refined and is now fully established such that all functions within the organisation now have confidence in it. The reasons for this are that it has reduced development times within the project framework: the number of tests has been reduced and the tracking of product developments has been made much easier and more visible. Moving outside the project framework has meant that a large number of functions have had to be involved in the design and development of the MDI.

This has had the knock-on effect of greater collaboration across functional boundaries. This was not the aim of the MDI but has been one of the great benefits in that it has become a vehicle that has forced people to exchange ideas and discuss problems. Perhaps the key element of it all is the translation from laboratory samples to production trials and full production. The production people are now much more closely linked in at the initial stages of the R&D development and the transition from development to full production appears to be much smoother.

Key findings

The work with BBA provides numerous lessons but the key one is how a well-thought-out product development strategy can be a major influence for corporate well-being. This is closely followed by the need for a good management information system for this type of development work.

11.3   Continental Sports Ltd (Huddersfield, UK)

- *Introduction of a structured idea and concept generation methodology.*
- *Introduction of a stage-gate progressing process.*
- *Adoption of best practice NPD approach.*

Company background

Continental Sports Ltd is a small business based in Huddersfield employing some 80 people. It has two main streams of business activity. The first is the supply of sports and gymnasium equipment into world-class activities. Continental was the approved supplier to the recent British Trampoline Federation Championships and has been used in world, European and National championship events. The second is the supply of equipment for school sports, especially gymnasiums.

Key issues

Continental is very good at the design and development process but has major problems with shifting markets. In the first market, which is the international events, it is being exposed to more and more competition, with national organisers gravitating towards suppliers from the country in which the event is being organised. In the second category, which is supply to schools, the Local Management of Schools Initiative (LMSI) has caused the company tremendous problems in that prior to this it would deal with a single person in a local authority and would cover some 200 or so local authorities. The LMSI means that the company now has to access some 44,000 individual schools and this is proving to be a major problem. Continental's sales have remained fairly static over the past three or four years despite various attempts to try to move this stuck turnover.

Continental wanted to work out ways of analysing and diversifying its markets. The work involved a comprehensive review of the whole business, with particular emphasis in two areas:

- Business generation, particularly new business generation.
- Complete review of the product development processes.

It became apparent that one of the major problems that the company faced was the syndrome of 'We have tried that before and it didn't work'. One of the things that had not been tried was to let the people who were doing the NPD work determine what needed to be done. When this was pointed out, the company agreed that it was worth a try.

A product development review team was set up consisting of the Sales Manager, the Production Manager, the Design Engineer and the Estimator. Time was spent educating them into best practice approaches to NPD. This was done in a series of seminars held in the evenings and focusing on the needs specifically outlined by Continental Sports. Several interesting things came out of all this activity in that there was a great desire by team members to be allowed to experiment with new ideas and new ways of doing things. They had detailed thoughts about how they could diversify the business, what were the key core competencies in the organisation and how these could be exploited.

During one of the seminars a fundamental point was encountered, in that when this group presented items for consideration to the joint Managing Directors it did so in a very haphazard and probably ill-thought-out way. Things seen as being useful to do were not backed up with any analysis or any detail in terms of costs, potential, etc. Several development programmes were reviewed and it was felt that some had started without really undergoing an initial review to see whether they were viable in terms of the market and the business, although all were technically feasible within the organisation. The outcome of this was that the team members decided not to focus on specific product developments but to review the whole way in which they managed the introduction, development and marketing of their products.

A follow-up seminar looked at the ways that companies review market and business potential and then monitor the development process. Initially the team looked for specifics that could just be translated and used straight away. It was pointed out that a tailored approach was needed. The outcome was that of a business opportunity review sheet which had both a 'rough cut' approach and a 'detailed cut' approach. This covered business, market, development, production, market launch issues and the inclusion of 'gut feeling'. Together with the review sheet, a simple 1–10 scoring system was used within the sub-categories (within the main categories), the summation of which led to a go or no-go decision.

Tests were carried out on several past development programmes and seemed to correlate reasonably well between the successful and failed programmes. The use of a rough cut scoring system was a way of quickly weeding out developments that were not really viable or financially rewarding. Those that passed went on to the detailed cut analysis which would then determine which developments would go forward. The second part of this work was the process after this initial decision had been made. A development process flow sheet was drawn up which went through the complete process stages of design, prototype, test, production systems, pre-production, commercial trial and full production. Each stage had a go/no-go column, an estimated completion date column and then a series of dates for status reviews.

These two systems are now in constant use within the company and appear to have paid dividends. The company feels that it is much more likely to be focused on product developments that not only it can do technically, but are likely also to bring significant market rewards. The company feels much more comfortable with the way that the business is now developing in that the systematic approach can be seen by everybody and is driven by proper and careful analysis. It is also transparent in that everybody can see what it is that they are trying to do and whether the developments selected are viable throughout the whole development cycle.

Key findings

The use of a structured idea generation system coupled with a stage gate process covering concept generation to product launch has paid off handsomely for Continental.

11.4   Engineering Ltd (a confidential case study)

- *Introduction of a stage gate process with key performance measurements.*
- *Creating the appropriate culture for successful NPD.*
- *Total co-location of sales and engineering.*
- *Development of the company's personnel.*
- *Transfer of core skills, competencies and knowledge.*

Company background

The company is a component and subsystem company to the aerospace and defence industry with its origins in 1937. Its products are based on fairly high-technology mechanical engineering with electronics and software introduced in the 1980s. It generally achieves market differentiation by technological difficulty, mainly through its design capability. In one particular area of technology it has a world-wide reputation.

Traditionally it has been a contractor to the UK Ministry of Defence (MoD) and benefited from cost plus development contracts (which had given the technological differentiation) and single source production contracts. In the late 1980s the MoD embarked on a new initiative aimed at achieving value for money through the widespread use of competition. The later collapse of the Eastern bloc encouraged a reduction in defence spending. The effect of these changes was threefold:

- A loss of the direct funding of leading edge R&D.
- A loss of easy networking that was facilitated by the MoD-sponsored R&D.
- Exposure to the pressures of competition with inevitable reduction in margins.

None of this was unique to the company, the effects being widespread across the defence industry.

Having been successful in the past, the company was relatively 'well off' in terms of programmes and technologies. It attempted to expand into new products and markets and, to quote, 'made a mess of it, especially the time/cost issue and also in technical excellence'. There was a loss of skills as a result of an over-dependence on new blood with experience being side-lined. In 1988 an engineer who had been working in sales and project management was moved back to engineering to try and resolve the problems that the new environment was posing.

Key issues

The first issue was the question of deciding on which projects to work. The company introduced a stage gate process to decide on projects and to make sure of their potential in terms of market, technological difficulty, the risk/reward equation, the conducting of proper estimates, the proper assessment of competition and who should be involved. This introduced a wider informed view into the selection process. To support it, a culture change had to be introduced where the technical staff would only work on projects that had been authorised through the formal procedures. This had to be an intelligent culture where a line was drawn between being properly helpful and supportive to sales and manufacturing colleagues while not allowing diversion of time or a bypass of the technical authorisation to occur.

During the 'free for all' period, the emphasis had been on novelty at the expense of the hard and relentless need to attend to the detail of the design to achieve not just something that works, but a product that fully meets the customers' requirement under all conditions of use. The ability to design a product that can be made repeatedly in production and at a price was also missing from some of the projects. The cause of these problems was seen to be due to the loss of experience, partly because of retirements and partly because of experienced staff being sidelined. To correct this, experienced staff were brought back into influence and authority. An important cultural issue was to ensure that experience was respected and consulted by management. This began to turn things around as the experienced staff brought skills for immediate application and thus reduced the design quality problems that had been experienced. It also quickly began to provide training for the younger people who were willing to learn from the experience that was available to them. Some did not wish to learn and left the company but overall the company's skill base grew quickly. Over the following years the older, experienced staff progressively retired but the knowledge was by then embedded.

The company identified that the key differentiating factors between success and failure of a new product development project were team play and the engineering skills. The shortage of experienced and fully trained staff had resulted in authority for the detail of the engineering process being controlled at a high level (the Chief Designer). This resulted in a very high workload at that level and a constraint on the throughput of engineering work. During this time, the company's focus changed from an emphasis on estimating and planning to picking the correct team members and building them into effective units. As engineering skill built up, project responsibility was pushed down the authority level, away from senior managers to the project team leaders.

The company restructured the Engineering Group into two project groups with cross-functional support teams. Clearly defined terms of reference were written which were available to everybody. These were not simple job descriptions but specific requirements in terms of actions and responsibilities. These terms of reference were used to nominate project team leaders covering about 80 active projects of which 15 were major developments.

The key issue of this team-based activity was the company's culture. A deliberate policy of creating a non-threatening environment was adopted to allow for quick and effective resolution of problems. Key performance monitoring measures were established, together with clearly visible meetings and good team spirit. Project responsibility pushed the engineers into interfacing with the customers and demanded that they had a more commercial-based approach and knowledge. The company introduced a programme of commercial training for all engineers which significantly improved their negotiating capability.

The final piece in the whole of this jigsaw was the introduction of co-location of sales and engineering. This was established and was 'forced' into operation by the stage gating process described earlier. This allowed positioning in the market-place as the technology/sales balance could be defined and the company could sell what could be created and not what it had got.

Key findings

The key lessons to be learned are that successful product engineering depends on skill and team working. Skill is a combination of innate talent, learning and experience. Managers must ensure that a blend of youth and experience is achieved and a fundamental of this is a culture of respect (both ways). Team work is vital and without a cohesive team there is little chance of achieving the technical and commercial goals of the project. Management's role is to pick the team and monitor its performance with an awareness of team as well as technical skills.

Delegation of project responsibility had a great benefit in that it enabled many projects to be successfully run in parallel, thus maximising the throughput of the organisation. It also provided young engineers with an exciting career path that got them involved with customers and the commercial realities of the business. This raised other issues in that some sales and marketing staff tended to regard the customer as their possession and were inclined to accompany engineers on visits. The problems were twofold in that the resource of two people was wasted on visiting customers and, secondly, the technical people tended to be set as second class. These issues are still being worked on at the present time.

While co-location of the sales and engineering functions has been of great benefit, the problem of harmonisation of remuneration packages remains. Sales people in the UK expect the 'so-called' perks of cars, including servicing, but it is not sensible to give every engineer a car. The problem remains, although the Chancellor is gradually reducing it! Sales staff normally do have a large amount of business commitment outside normal working hours which the car goes some way to offset. However, engineers also have increasing hours as the throughput increases for a fixed number of people. The solution has been to pay engineers a flat rate overtime payment as compensation. The situation is, however, not satisfactory and harmonisation of remuneration is needed within a single new product development function.

11.5   Lantor (UK) Ltd (Bolton, UK)

- *Introduction of a rigorous product development selection system.*
- *Integrating the customer into the development process.*
- *Focusing on a product 'Champion' approach as opposed to formal teams.*

Company background

Lantor (UK) Ltd develops and manufactures non-woven fabric-based products predominantly for industrial, medical and military use. The company has 65 employees. Although there have been improvements made over the past few years, Lantor still strongly believed that its problems in product development stemmed from the need for more effective selection and monitoring of developments.

The work with Lantor covered a comprehensive review of their product development activities and process. This has covered the areas of:

- ISO 9001 approval.
- Practical, day-to-day operations.
- Product development strategy.

Key issues

It was estimated that the company accepted 60–70% of all enquiries. The success rate of these projects was thought to be around 10% and although theoretically low was considered quite acceptable. However, it was felt that better projects could be selected and better information gleaned at the start of projects. The large number of projects prevented the use of teams. It was felt by some that there was a general lack of contact between departments relying on the project leaders to gather relevant company members together as required, on an ad hoc basis. Teams were not formally formed for developments. Team members were pulled into the project when they were required (some 70–75 projects are live at any one time in the company).

Lantor wished to establish ISO 9000 for the development process. An initial and somewhat lengthy new product development monitoring procedure was honed down to their current document. There is a need at present to develop an implementation strategy. Lantor does not formally measure the success of its products.

Key findings

The first key finding for Lantor was the use of a rigorous system to select the 'right' development at the outset. The second was the realisation that the use of product 'Champions', as opposed to formal teams, was right for the company. Being a small company with many development programmes, this was seen as the best management process.

The third key finding was that of customer integration. Surepress is a padding bandage containing super-absorbent fibre used under a compression stretch bandage in the treatment of venous ulcers. It was developed for ConvaTec, an important new international medical customer, who had identified a strong need for the product in a market with little competition. The super-absorbent fibres give the product enhanced absorbent capacity over competitors' products reducing the need to change the dressing. The fibres swell and gel with the uptake of liquid preventing the exudate from moving under the compression bandage and create more localised pressure which was thought to be beneficial.

Lantor is currently one of only a few companies who have adopted the use of super-absorbent fibres for medical products and this has raised its profile as a medical supplier.

The product fitted well with Lantor's expertise in utilising existing technology and equipment. Despite the long, straight, coarse nature of the fibres, which made them difficult to hold together, there were few technical problems experienced in the development of the product using the new raw material.

ConvaTec launched Surepress at a show in September 1995 but did not market it until January 1996. Surepress is a CE-marked product complying with the European Medical Device Directive. Timing was not as critical as achieving the product specification. The relationship with ConvaTec has proved particularly fruitful. It has become one of Lantor's major customers and there is a strong likelihood that the two companies will collaborate on further development projects.

The product was brought to market speedily and on time, successfully meeting the performance specification, sales and profit targets in the first year. It received a high priority within the company owing to its potential for profit generation and knock-on projects and was consequently well supported and resourced. There was a strong commitment to the project and notably close co-operation between production, quality assessment (QA) and R&D from the early stages.

The project benefited from strong project leadership and customer integration. Both Convatec and Lantor assigned project leaders to manage the development of the padding. The customer attended meetings regularly and was very clear as to what was required, setting clear guidelines and targets.

No formalised team was assigned to the project. However, regular meetings were held where members of the company were invited on an ad hoc basis. Personnel from Convatec, including purchasing, technical operations, logistics, R&D, QA, sales and marketing, regulatory affairs and clinical trials were involved with the project. The initial work on this project was carried out by Bolton Institute's School of Textile Studies and the supplier of the super-absorbent material was also involved in the early stages of the project.

11.6   Try & Lilly Ltd (Liverpool, UK)

- *Market-driven product development and innovation.*
- *Integrated, team-based management of the whole process.*
- *Acquisition-based NPD.*

Company background

Try & Lilly is a family-owned business established some 50 years ago. It is a specialist in high-quality hat manufacture and has two main product lines. The first one is uniform caps made for a wide variety of customers ranging from the military through to Railtrack and police forces, etc. The second group of products is of the deerstalker or country-wear type headwear. The company has been trying to diversify into other products and has developed a moulded hat which is worn, for example, by people serving on supermarket food counters. This product also has other outlets as lightweight summer headwear. Another diversification is into related products such as scarves and dressing gowns.

Key issues

The company was driven by the Managing Director (MD) who has all the technical and much of the commercial skills. This was, by the MD's own admittance, not a healthy situation. Its key future activities were effective development of new products and the move to team-based management to diffuse the dependence on the MD. Both these objectives have been achieved. The work has seen the company make a significant move in its new product portfolio. It has developed (by acquisition) a moulded hat that fits in with their traditional style but uses totally different technology from the traditional 'cut and sew'. The hat is designed on a CAD system and a mould is cut via a CNC machine. Specially treated fabric is vacuum formed onto the heated mould. The heat of the mould sets the resin impregnated cloth and produces the almost finished hat. This has become an extremely profitable product.

The authors took the company through a whole series of product development and team-based training programmes and this culminated in a recently completed two associate teaching company scheme. One associate concentrated on the marketing and development of new products while the other associate concentrated on the operational activities to support the new products as they come on stream.

Key findings

The key lessons that have been learnt include the need for a market-driven, team-based approach to product development. Within this is the need for a structured but not over-bureaucratic approach to the development process. The whole company is now heading toward a team-based management operation.

11.7   Wylex Ltd (Manchester, UK)

- *The use of a formal product planning process.*
- *Incremental development of products.*
- *Use of development procedures.*
- *Sticking to the 'core' businesses.*

Company background

Wylex (part of the Electrum Group) develops and manufactures electrical circuit protection equipment for a variety of markets. Consumer units (fuse boxes) form the mainstay of the business. Residual current devices (RCDs) represent about 14% of the business alongside industrial products such as protected socket outlets and 'specials' for one-off or niche applications.

Key issues

Wylex has a policy of keeping products 'in-house' from the largest down to the smallest components such as mouldings, press parts, screws, washers and all levels of assembly and sub-assembly. The success rate for new products is relatively high, but this is seen to be due less to a superior development process and more to the lack of risk taking in development. Most causes of failure are seen to be due to a failure in planning, especially when this relates to entering new markets with products. To date, Wylex has had two new product 'failures' and both entailed entering markets of which Wylex had little experience.

Key findings

The key findings for Wylex were the role that product planning played in determining success and also the use of procedures, especially at the market analysis and business planning stages.

Wylex introduced the NS range consumer unit to the market around six years ago and has easily met sales targets. The NS range falls into the category 'new product improvement' and provides a classic example of a company 'sticking to its knitting'. The reason the NS range has been so successful is due to success in the past with an equivalent product (the NN range). The NS range addressed shortfalls in the previous generation NN range, and the product was supported by a full market launch.

Part V

Useful contacts and addresses

12

Useful contacts and addresses

Key: indicating the organisation's main activities.

B	Business support	**D**	Design	**G**	'Green'
E	Education	**I**	Innovation	**M**	Management
P	Product development	**Q**	Quality	**S**	Service

Association for Service Management International   B/S/M/P
Pim WHR Bonsel, Begoniastraat 30, B-3930 Hamont-Achel, Belgium
Tel.: 32 11 66 52 27; Fax: 32 11 66 52 72

British Chambers of Commerce   B
Manning House, 22 Carlisle Place, London, SW1P 1JA, UK
Tel.: +44 (0)171 565 2000; Fax: +44 (0)171 565 2049

British Standards Institute   Q
389 Chiswick High Street, London W4 4AL, UK
Tel.: +44 (0)845 608 9000; www.bsi.org.uk

Business Link Directorate   B
St Mary's House, c/o Moorfoot, Sheffield S1 4FQ, UK
Tel.: +44 (0)114 259 7504

Concurrent Engineering Research Center   D/P
Drawer 2000, West Virginia University, Morgantown, WV 26506, USA
Tel.: 1 304 293 7726; Fax: 1 304 293 7541; E-mail jrs@cerc.wvu.wvnet.edu

Department of Trade and Industry   B/I/P
4D55, 1 Victoria Street, London SW1H 0ET, UK
Tel.: +44 (0)171 215 3916, (0)171 215 2877; www.dti.gov.uk

Department of Trade and Industry Innovation Unit   I/P
151 Buckingham Palace Road, London SW1W 9SS, UK
E-mail 10040.731@compuserve.com

Design Council   D/P
34 Bow Street, London WC2E 7DL, UK
Tel.: +44 (0)171 420 5200; Fax: +44 (0)171 420 5300

Design Policy Unit   D/P
1 Victoria Street, London SW1 0ET, UK
Tel.: +44 (0)171 215 3855; Fax: +44 (0)171 215 3935

ECODESIGN TU Vienna   D/G/I/P
www.ecodesign.at/ecodesign__eng/literat/index.htm

Engineering Management Society (Institute of Electrical and Electronic Engineers)   D/E/M/P
45 Hoes Lane, PO Box 1331, Piscataway
NJ 08855 1331, USA
Tel.: 1 908 981 0060; Fax: 1 908 981 9667

Institute of Management   B/E/M
3rd Floor, 2 Savoy Court, London WC2R 0EZ, UK
Tel.: +44 (0)171 497 0550; Fax: +44 (0)171 497 0463; E-mail savoy@inst-mgt.org.uk; www.inst-mgt.org.uk

International Society for Professional Innovation Management   E/I/P
Technology Management, Eindhoven University of Technology, PO Box 513, 5600 MB Eindhoven, The Netherlands
Tel.: 31 40 247 2170/2372; Fax: 31 40 246 8054; E-mail bdokan@popserver.tue.nl; www.wirehub.nl/ispim

National Center for Environmental Decision-Making Research   G
Oak Ridge National Laboratory, Tennessee Valley Authority, University of Tennessee

Product Development and Management Association   M/P
401 North Michigan Avenue, Chicago, IL 60611 4267, USA
Tel.: 1 800 232 5241 and 1 312 527 6644; Fax: 1 31312 527 6729; E-mail: PDMA@sba.com; www.pdma.org

R&D Research Unit   E/I/M/P
Manchester Business School, Manchester M15 6PB, UK
Tel.: +44 (0)161 275 6338; Fax: +44 (0)161 275 7143; E-mail: j.butler@f52.mbs.ac.uk

Research and Development Society   I/M/P
20-22 Queensbury Place, London SW7 2DZ, UK

Tel.: +44 (0)171 581 8333; Fax: +44 (0)171 823 9409; E-mail: info@iob.primex.co.uk

Research and Development Society (Special Interest Group)   I/P
Dr Iain Simpson, AI Cambridge Ltd, London Road, Pampisford, Cambridge CB2 4EE, UK
Tel.: +44 (0)1223 834420

Technology Management Group   E/G/I/M/P
School of Engineering, Liverpool John Moores University, Byrom Street, Liverpool L3 3AF, UK
Tel.: +44 (0)151 231 2384; Fax: +44 (0)151 207 2753; E-mail: i.barclay@livjm.ac.uk; www.eng.livjm.ac.uk/TechnologyManagement

Training and Enterprise Councils National Council   B/E/I/M
Westminster Tower, 3 Albert Embankment, London SE1 7SX, UK
Tel.: +44 (0)171 735 0010; Fax: +44 (0)171 735 0090; E-mail: info@tec.co.uk

Appendices

Appendix 1

The NPD integrating activities model

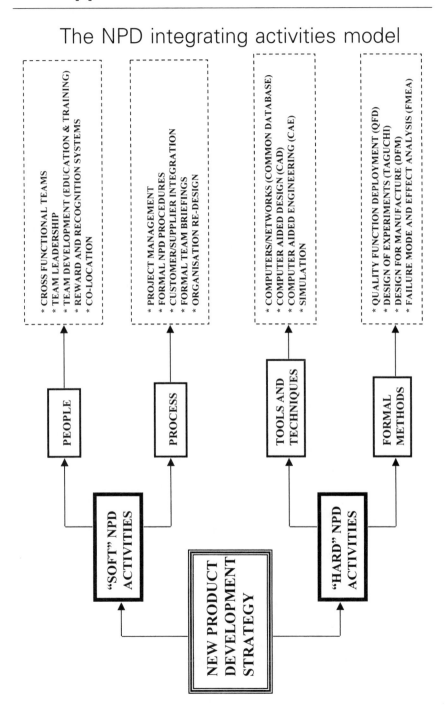

Appendix 2

The NPD process model

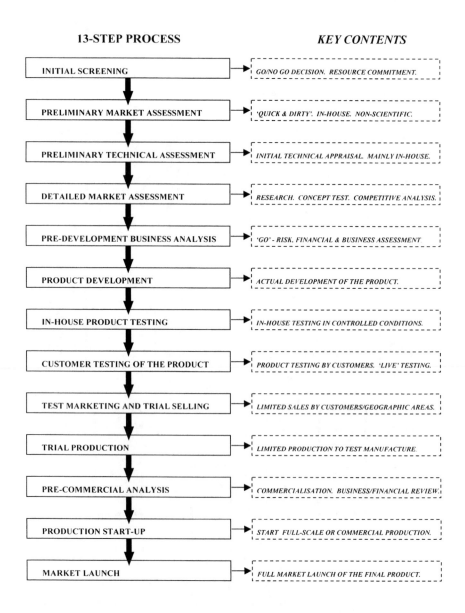

13-STEP PROCESS	KEY CONTENTS
INITIAL SCREENING	*GO/NO GO DECISION. RESOURCE COMMITMENT.*
PRELIMINARY MARKET ASSESSMENT	*'QUICK & DIRTY'. IN-HOUSE. NON-SCIENTIFIC.*
PRELIMINARY TECHNICAL ASSESSMENT	*INITIAL TECHNICAL APPRAISAL. MAINLY IN-HOUSE.*
DETAILED MARKET ASSESSMENT	*RESEARCH. CONCEPT TEST. COMPETITIVE ANALYSIS.*
PRE-DEVELOPMENT BUSINESS ANALYSIS	*'GO' - RISK, FINANCIAL & BUSINESS ASSESSMENT*
PRODUCT DEVELOPMENT	*ACTUAL DEVELOPMENT OF THE PRODUCT.*
IN-HOUSE PRODUCT TESTING	*IN-HOUSE TESTING IN CONTROLLED CONDITIONS.*
CUSTOMER TESTING OF THE PRODUCT	*PRODUCT TESTING BY CUSTOMERS. 'LIVE' TESTING.*
TEST MARKETING AND TRIAL SELLING	*LIMITED SALES BY CUSTOMERS/GEOGRAPHIC AREAS.*
TRIAL PRODUCTION	*LIMITED PRODUCTION TO TEST MANUFACTURE.*
PRE-COMMERCIAL ANALYSIS	*COMMERCIALISATION. BUSINESS/FINANCIAL REVIEW.*
PRODUCTION START-UP	*START FULL-SCALE OR COMMERCIAL PRODUCTION.*
MARKET LAUNCH	*FULL MARKET LAUNCH OF THE FINAL PRODUCT.*

Appendix 3

NPD integrating activities and process relationship with product's complexities

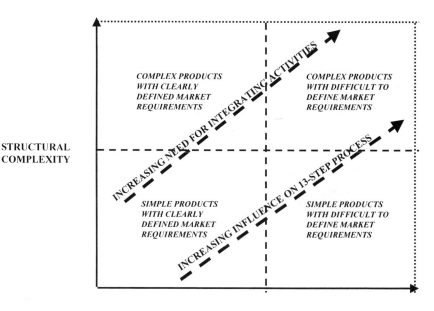

Appendix 4

Reviewing NPD strategy

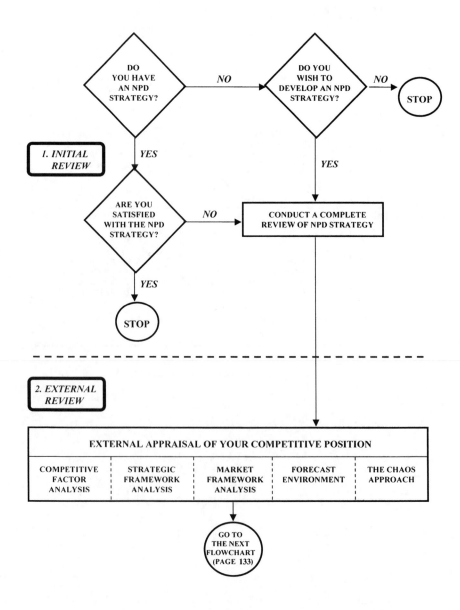

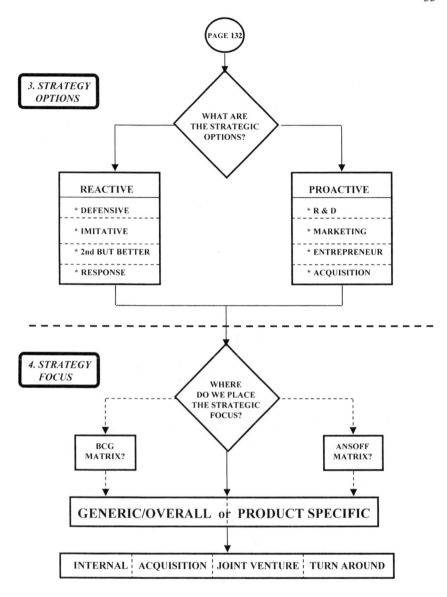

Appendix 5

Measuring development performance

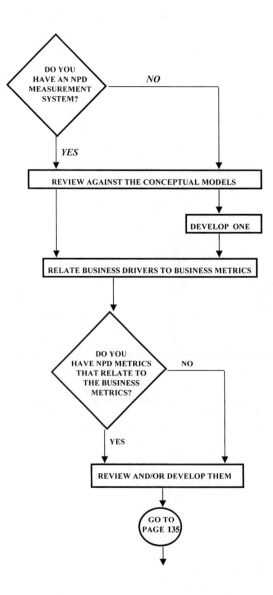

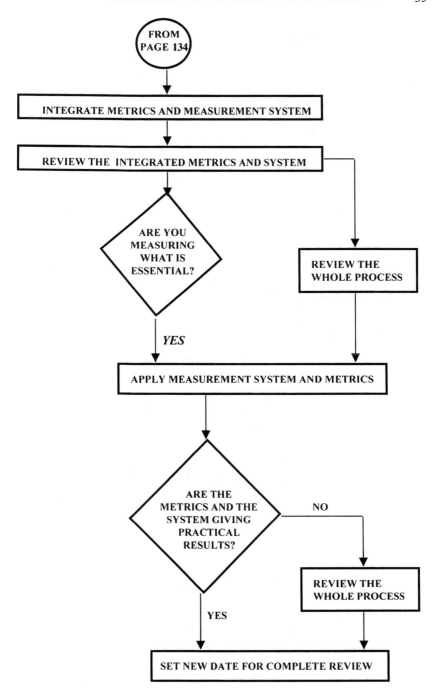

Appendix 6

Improving NPD performance

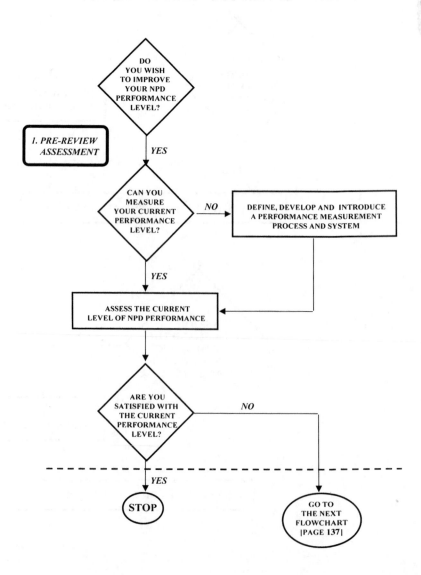

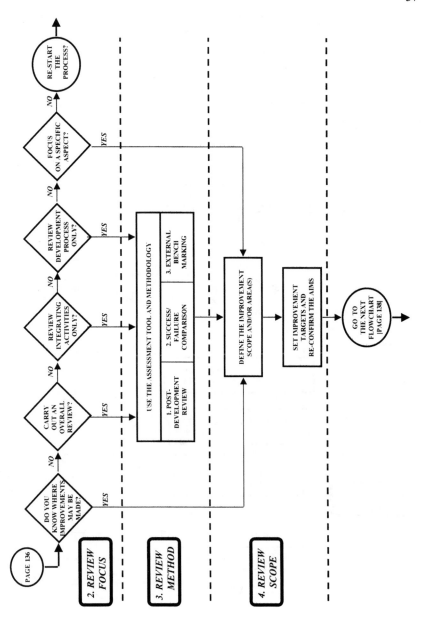

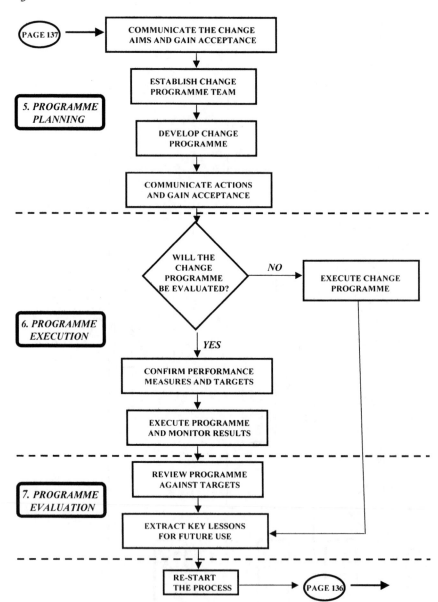

Index